The 11 Commandments and 7 Cardinal Sins of Selling a Business

Second edition

A pragmatic guide to achieving
a premium price for your
business

ROBERT GODDARD

DEDICATION

Life is a series of encounters with people – sometimes for a short time, sometimes for a lifetime. This book is dedicated to family, friends and business colleagues that I have had or still have the joy of knowing and have learnt so much from.

In particular, the book is dedicated to my four children, Tom, Josh, Haydn and Phoenix, who give my life meaning, significance and purpose. I feel privileged to be a father to such wonderful children. They have enriched my life in countless ways and been a blessing to me through the good times and the bad.

CONTENTS

A journey of 1,000 miles starts with a single step.

Lau Tzu, Chinese philosopher (604 BC - 531 BC)

FOREWORD

Winning at sport and winning in business have many cross-overs. Preparation, persistence and the desire to be the best in your chosen field are all fundamental to performance excellence. The principles shared in Rob's book are designed to help you increase the hidden value and maximise the potential within your business.

Olympic Medal Winners

Roger Black MBE
Steve Backley OBE

Robert Goddard

VIII

INTRODUCTION

"In the beginning"

Few are given the blueprint to running a business successfully and this is especially so for planning an attractive exit from that same business. When is the right time to sell? How do you make sure that your business passes into the right hands? What is a fair price for your business? What is the likelihood of selling? These are all perfectly reasonable questions, but rarely ever answered satisfactorily. This book is designed to provide you with all the tips, guidance and knowledge you will need to have not only to sell your business, but to earn its maximum value. I want to share the "secrets" with you that I have learned from the experience I have gained since 2002, having been responsible for the successful sale of hundreds of businesses.

It's a "dog eat dog" world out there and many would not want to share their knowledge with others out of fear that they might lose a competitive edge in business. The intent of this book is the complete reverse. I want you to be informed and equipped to tackle what can often be the roller-coaster ride of selling a business. I will dispel some of the myths surrounding business sales and instead provide you with pragmatic advice for what is likely to be one of the major events in your life.

Preparation is the key for a successful exit and yet so many business owners fail to plan properly for this. If you were selling your house, you would undoubtedly prepare it for viewings. You would make it tidy, attractive, have all the relevant paperwork available and be prepared for any tricky questions regarding your property. Yet, surprisingly many business owners fail to attend to these basics before they meet potential buyers and are consequently at a significant negotiation disadvantage.

In a survey of their business customers, the private bank, Coutts & Co. found that only 7% of owners who marketed their business for sale actually sold. Harvard Business School had previously undertaken a much larger scale survey and found that only 30% of businesses sold. I daresay that, somewhere between these two, the truth lies.

My aim with this book is to help you to successfully sell your business for a premium price, and at the same time make the process as smooth as possible.

So why would any business owner sell their treasured possession? The life to which they have given birth, nurtured and taken care of over many years?

In my experience, there are four key reasons that trigger the sale of a business:

1. Time – Or rather, the lack of it, to do the things you really want to do in life. Life is so much more than working 70+ hours a week. The first one in the office and the last to leave does not make for a contented, well-rounded existence. A situation where you are never out of contact with the office, thanks to the technological advancements in communication, is not a healthy one. Business owners usually have the resources to take many holidays a year but find it extremely difficult to take time out completely. When, or if they do, manage to take time off they bring their smart-phone on holiday too, unable to let go of regular contact with the office and afraid of missing those all-important emails that demand instant attention. But are they so important in the greater scheme of how you value your life? The old adage counsels that "you can't buy time, only spend it."

So selling your business can help to provide the capital for you to finish one chapter in your life and start a new one; one that provides you with the time to achieve many other things in life. One of my clients told me that the first thing he wanted to do after selling his business was to restore his Dad's old car, a 1936 Morris Tourer. It had been in storage for over 30 years and my client never had the time to dedicate to the much needed restoration work. We sold his business and when I visited him a few months later the first thing that greeted my eye was the vintage car sitting proudly in the garage, in the process of being restored. My client sat proudly with it, looking much more relaxed and content. For him, selling his business was a natural move in order to make room in his life for other, more enriching ways to spend his time.

2. Manager vs. Entrepreneur – If you have set up a business from new, it is often an exciting and dynamic experience. As time goes by and the business grows, staff are employed and new systems are introduced. Then the excitement starts to give way to more routine and bureaucratic, but equally important, considerations such as employment law, health & safety, and so on. These new considerations seem a thousand miles away from your original business idea and can take hold of your focus and energy like an invasive vine. It can feel like you are imprisoned in your office, slavishly dealing with emails and phone calls. As a result, many business owners feel that the fun goes out of running their own business. It has somehow gravitated from a fast moving entrepreneurial environment to one that has trapped you in a management role that is weighed down with bureaucracy, staff issues, and just "stuff" that seems utterly unrelated to your original entrepreneurial inspiration.

Is it any wonder that after several years, business owners start to resent these inevitable changes that arise with a successful, expanding business? Who would not want to return to an environment and routine that is more flexible and exciting? An IT services client once said to me, "the reason I'm selling my business Rob is that, to be honest, I don't much care for managing staff." It wasn't because he didn't like or appreciate his staff, he simply wasn't cut out to manage them. Some business owners are initiators and others are maintainers of a business. One is not better than the other, they are just different skill sets. As owner/managers, being self-aware is the key. If you know what you excel at, life is much more enjoyable and rewarding – even more so if you are also aware of what tends to block your creative and dynamic entrepreneurial talents.

Many of my former clients have returned back to business life as a "Business Angel," investing in several businesses rather than just one. This has allowed them to have an enjoyable degree of involvement, but not the responsibility of running things day to day. They enjoy the cut and thrust of being an entrepreneur without the "mill-stone," as many see it, of managing staff, systems and processes.

3. Change of lifestyle – This is linked inextricably with the two points above, centring on wanting a new focus in life and having the resources to undertake it. Many business owners are financially comfortable, but are seeking to make the future more certain for themselves and their families. They want to fill it with things they have always wanted to do but never had the time for. An opportunity to live abroad perhaps, with a slower pace of life and simply time to enjoy "the present." This resonates with my own story. My exit plan is to live on a Greek Island and to teach English part-time by the time I'm 55 years old. Some years ago I qualified under the TEFL scheme. I will also buy a Double Decker bus to convert to a mobile language school. My wife Liz said to me, "what happens when the bus breaks down?"

"Easy" I replied, "It can then be our villa in Greece!" I love the prospect of being able to be flexible with changing situations and to welcome the changes they bring to our lives.

4. Change of investment lifecycle – You'll see from the graph below that every business is somewhere on the growth line. For all owners this means being faced with the decision to reinvest in their business several times during their ownership.

In the graph below, the owner created a start-up business, enjoying high growth in the early years. But at some point the financial performance of the business plateaued. It does for every business. If you are aware of a business that has a never ending growth trajectory, please let me know – I would like to buy it! At the point of performance starting to level off, the decision to re-invest or sell emerges. Do you invest your own retained profits, attract a new investor or simply borrow the capital required? You may decide to set up a new office or develop a new product. There are many alternatives to consider.

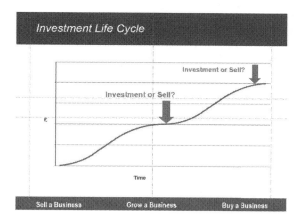

The decision in the example above was to fund future growth, whereupon the cycle begins once more so that at some point in the future, once again the decision to invest or sell emerges. As an owner you are presented with this choice several times over the lifetime of your business.

I'm often asked by owners how they will know when the "right" time to sell is. This is an impossible question to answer with any accuracy. It's perhaps easier to answer the question, "when is it a bad time to sell a business? " Selling at a peak in performance is often the wrong time to sell. This is because buyers are likely to say, "Your business has maxed out so I'm not paying you a premium price" and "Where is the growth going to come from?" Sellers of businesses need to ensure they leave "oxygen" in the deal for a buyer. By that I mean, attractive growth prospects for the future, allowing the would-be acquirer to benefit from another growth phase post-acquisition. Buyers understandably want to have their initial investment repaid as quickly as possible and achieve "quick wins." Think about it for a moment. If the potential buyer needs to invest considerable monies to grow the business, that is likely to mean less money available to buy your shares.

On the other hand, a common criticism of business owners is that they keep hold of their business for too long, always waiting for another year or two of more growth. I have lost count of the number of times that owners have said to me, "I wish I had sold a few years ago!" Some have even died before they got the opportunity to make that decision. Nature made that decision for them, often leaving their affairs and the business in a mess.

The decision to sell your business should not be predicated purely on when it's thought the maximum amount of money can be generated. It should also be based on your personal life goals and plans. How does the sale of your business fit into those aspects of your life? There is often the temptation to put things off for another year or two; until ill-health or a decrease in the fortunes of your business force you into considering selling. Neither of these situations help you achieve a good price for your business, since circumstances are dictating to you the timing for sale.

It is far better to prepare your business and plan now, making your company "sale ready." Many businesses are not ready for sale. The following is a list of common criticisms that buyers have regarding vendor businesses:

- Inadequate succession planning
- Owner-reliance
- A single client representing more than 20% of overall turnover
- Exposure to a volatile supply chain
- Lack of, or out-of-date, employee contracts
- Inconsistent internal systems and processes
- Unrealistic price aspirations
- Sellers not knowing their financials
- Poor credit control
- No clear picture as to where future growth will come from
- Intellectual Property has not been commercially protected

This is not an exhaustive list, but it should give you a flavour of some of the common areas of risk, as the buyer sees it.

For buyers, the rule to remember is that:

INCREASED RISK = LOWER OFFER

Your role as seller is to help reduce (perceived) risk for the buyer. This will help you form a platform to increase price and improve exit terms. The list above should give you a good checklist to examine your own business. How many apply to your business?

The following 11 Commandments will also help unpack the issues involved in selling your business for its true value.

XVI

The 11 Commandments and 7 Cardinal Sins of Selling a Business

Second edition

CHAPTER 1

Commandment #1
"Create competitive tension between buyers"

It seems obvious to most people that if you have a choice of potential buyers, you are more likely to drive up your asking price. However, you would be amazed at the number of times I have spoken with business owners who are only speaking with one prospective buyer! This is with the mistaken notion that it will save them time and money. The reverse is actually true; it will cost them significantly. The lack of competitive tension will mean that large chunks of time are spent running around for a potential buyer, gathering data, making financial forecasts, supplying yet more information, only to discover that several months down the line their original sweet overtures become silent and communication fades away. The so-called buyer either finds another target company to purchase, or can even re-emerge as a competitor against you, armed with all that very helpful information and data you kindly provided to them previously.

I met a business owner of a recruitment company on the South coast who proudly said he didn't need anyone's assistance in selling his business, since he had recently received a phone call from one of his competitors making an attractive indicative offer on his business. In fact, he proudly told me, they were in his business this week taking a look at the database and systems, before they moved forward in the sale process.

I asked why they would need to buy his business if he had already given them open access to all his commercially sensitive data, including their own login and passwords. There was silence from him as the penny dropped. He had been seduced by a seemingly high offer from a much larger business in his sector. They never bought his business; in fact, they never progressed their offer. I suspect, however, that data which had taken over 20 years to amass was downloaded and copied by that competitor.

> **Tip #1 – Never let any buyer be the "only show in town." If you do, it will cost you at the negotiating table. Instead, make sure you meet at least 6 potential strategic buyers. The price will rise and the exit terms will improve for you.**

I have found that at least 100 buyers need to be approached to generate meetings with half a dozen potential buyers. It's hard work, takes time and commitment, but it pays off in the end, with the sale value and deal structure you are seeking. Make sure too that you research possible international buyers. More and more companies from overseas are buying UK businesses, particularly from India and China. China's richest man bought a 92% stake in Sunseeker Yachts recently. Twenty years ago, who would have believed that someone from Communist China would have bought a global luxury brand? Your research needs to be extensive and uncompromising and may take you many weeks to undertake, but it pays handsomely if you invest the time.

I once sold a Scottish aerosol business to a Russian company with comparable products. Despite the Russian business being much larger and in the same sector, my client had never come across them. Some business owners believe they have a thorough knowledge of their market and who operates within it. It's a perception and is rarely a reality. Therefore, as part of the research to identify would-be acquirers, you should look internationally as well as the home market. Ever increasingly, companies from countries such as China, India, Middle East and Russia are buying UK businesses as part of their global growth plans. As a business seller you ought to be in contact with organisations in some of these regions. If you do not have access to these sorts of research resources, find someone who does.

A former colleague of mine once said that paying a third party to undertake the buyer research was "sleep" money to the seller. Meaning, that after a business sale had completed, the seller could sleep at night, knowing there wasn't a better acquirer or deal out there. To be comprehensive and uncompromising in your research is essential to a successful outcome for you and will give you peace of mind, protecting you from wondering whether you could have received more money for your business. In my own business we have found that identifying 20/30 prospective buyers is insufficient but, for the majority of sellers, between 80 and 120 is optimum. Clearly, your business may only be one of a handful of companies globally that do what you do and so you may think there is no way anyone could find 80+ prospective buyers for your business.

However, what about complementary businesses to yours, looking to expand into your sector? By complementary I mean businesses that provide different products and services to yours, but sell into a similar client base to your own. By acquiring your company, they automatically diversify their offering. Furthermore, by combining two client bases they give a perfect platform to cross-sell and upsell. This is often referred to as "synergistic fit." Some clients come to me and say, "I have a buyer already, can you just negotiate a deal for me?" My first response is to ask for sight of the "offer." Of course, rarely is there ever anything in writing, it nearly always amounts to a conversation and sometimes not even a sale price or outline deal structure. This is not an offer, simply an expression of apparent interest.

The first thing to do with an expression of interest is to get the potential buyer to put it in writing, with a price and a proposed structure of a deal. Will they buy 100% of your shares or is it a trade and asset deal? Will they pay in cash on completion day or are they proposing to defer payment over a period of time? Are they offering part shares, part cash? When would they seek to complete a deal with you? How do they propose funding an acquisition?

Whilst they are formulating this you need to create a "pool" of other interested parties for your business – at least 80 – to ensure you maximise your sale price. Creating competitive tension is crucial to the price you eventually receive for your business. Above all, don't be in a rush to get into an exclusive situation with a potential buyer.

Instead, if you do have someone who has expressed some sort of interest in buying your business, this is good, but offer them "1st mover advantage." Explain to them that you plan to speak with other potential buyers, but they now have an opportunity to get ahead of the market, to make you an offer you surely can't refuse! Say it with some humour, but they must know that you intend speaking with other interested parties. Why wouldn't you?

Please see Case Study 1 on page 9. Through competitive tension in the process we managed to increase the original offer by 72%.

Since the collapse of Lehman Brothers in 2008 where the financial world went into chaos, it has been a buyer's market, not a seller's market. Anyone who tells you differently is not being honest with you so be careful where you seek advice when you come to selling your business. Therefore, you must, at all cost, create a competitive environment within which to sell your business and switch the dynamics in your favour.

In my experience of successfully selling hundreds of businesses, the following holds true in almost every case:

100 prospects lead to
25 interested parties lead to
6 meetings lead to
3 offers lead to
1 sale

At one of my Masterclasses, a delegate said that he had had over 30 years' experience in sales and marketing and that these conversion rates are generic across most sectors. It's therefore not just true of selling a business, but of many other industry sectors too. One other advantage of establishing a competitive market place is that you will feel more confident about the process, especially in negotiation meetings. Potential buyers will sense that "vibe" from you and it will help strengthen your negotiating posture in meetings. What you want to communicate is that you don't need to sell your business but, if you did, there are several people with whom you are negotiating. Trust me, serious buyers will "sharpen their pencil" with this news and will want to move things forward with you without delay.

The competitive tension you build remains throughout the process, until the sale proceeds are in your bank account. It is especially important once you enter a phase of the process called "Due Diligence." This is a part of the sale process in which the prospective buyer checks that what they think they are buying is in fact what they are getting. They will inspect the commercial, legal and financial aspects of your business before paying you for your shares. Typically, it's a 60-day period, but this can vary.

Most buyers use this stage to help them reduce their original offer, alleging that it isn't right, or that it does not reflect what they had been led to believe. There is no advantage to the seller in the "Due Diligence" process. Offers are never increased by the buyer after completion of it. The best you can hope for is no change from the original offer. However, if you have created a competitive market, you still have other potential buyers you can revert to if the chosen buyer starts being unreasonable. Yes, you will need to wait for the period of exclusivity to elapse, usually up to 60 days, but nevertheless, you have that choice, and it is worth keeping in touch with a pool of potential buyers during this time.

An IT client of mine tried to sell their business themselves a couple of years prior to coming to me; it was a disaster, they told me. They had only spoken with one buyer, a larger US company, but the indicative offer they accepted was above what they had hoped for and so they moved forward eagerly into "Due Diligence." The offer started coming down and things that the American company said they wouldn't do started to increase, such as changing the contracts of the staff. They then declared that they would do. This inconsistency nearly drove my client into exhaustion with nervous stress. Quite incredibly, the "Due Diligence" took eighteen months of exhausting meetings, telephone calls, requests for further information, and so on. Eventually the seller pulled out because they couldn't see an end to it all and were astounded that a potential buyer could go back on their word. They came to me wanting to know how they could have avoided this situation in the future. The answer is simple: don't talk with just one buyer, and when you do find a buyer you want to sell to, make sure you agree to no more than 60 days' exclusivity for the buyer to conduct their "Due Diligence" on your business.

One Buyer is No Buyer! A seller cannot expect to sell at market value if their business is not exposed to the market and given a competitive run to the final sale. Never, ever, give a buyer the huge advantage that they are "the only show in town."

Case Study 1
Pioneering small business bought
by market leader WBC Ltd

Creating competition is a key element in maximising the sale value of a business; it's part of our corporate presentation. The reason for this is that, to coin the old phrase, "every business is worth different amounts to different acquirers". Our client, Canby Ltd was established in 2002 as a carbon neutral company with a truly ethical ethos in all areas of business. It became a leading supplier of premium quality, environmentally friendly jute and cotton bags to business customers. Products are manufactured from natural fibres, sourced from ethically certified factories. They have a varied client base including prestigious brands such as the Eden Project, Fortnum & Mason, the Victoria & Albert Museum, The National Gallery and English Heritage.

Following our initial engagement in 2011, we took the company to market in February and completed the sale in 9 months. Our marketing plan involved identifying potential purchasers and then carrying out a synergistic profiling exercise that resulted in the 58 companies that formed our Calling List. We made nearly 900 calls to these companies over a two month calling period. This highly proactive marketing approach generated meetings with six companies and we received three indicative offers for our client's business. The spread of offers, from lowest to highest was over 250%. The result was the sale of Canby to WBC (Wine Box Company) Limited – a packaging company sharing Canby's ethical and environmental values.

WBC increasingly seeks ways to ensure its commitment to corporate responsibility and sustainability. The synergy between the two companies, both in terms of production and corporate values, demonstrates the importance of good research and profiling when taking a business to market.

Here is what David Gould, CEO of Canby has to say:

"Having Rob's team handle the marketing process has enabled me to continue running and growing the business over the past 10 months which has proven to be critical in terms of exit value".

Our client is now enjoying a welcome break with his young family before starting out on his next business venture. We wish him every success.

Deal Summary:
- 58 companies profiled and contacted
- 6 potential acquirer meetings
- 1 offer
  Deal completed in 9 months

CHAPTER 2

Commandment #2
"Be proactive in marketing your business"

Marketing your business to prospective buyers is not simply a matter of sending out some emails or posting an advert on the internet. True, it's relatively inexpensive, but of course your business will be for sale on the internet amongst tens of thousands of others, just like yours! So how do you make your business visible amongst the plethora of others for sale? How do you get the opportunity of buying your business across to relevant potential acquirers?

The answer lies in being highly proactive in approaching potential buyers. This means considerable time researching possible acquirers and then picking up the phone to have a conversation with them. To simply create an advert to put on the internet is unlikely to generate any or sufficient interest. You will need to go on the front foot and approach companies. This takes time and dedication, as most companies will decline or even reject your approach. Do not be discouraged; this is normal in selling a business. Typically, if you approach 100 companies, only six will want to meet with you and three of those will then go on to make offers on your business. You can easily make 1,000+ phone calls in your quest to find a buyer. There are no short cuts if you want to sell your business for a premium price. If you do not have the time, engage someone to do the work for you.

Your marketing material needs to be attractive to the eye, informative and focused on the future potential of your business. One common criticism of vendors is that they fail to paint a picture of the next few years of growth. If you can't forecast the next 3 years of your own business, how do you expect a buyer to. I am not talking about precise and highly detailed financial forecasting. I'm referring to a narrative whereby you describe the potential shape and size of your business over the next few years. There will naturally be some headline figures, but that narrative will substantiate where the growth is likely to come from, and when.

> **Tip #2 - Approach the investment community such as Private Equity, Venture Capital and Business Angel networks, all of whom have an ever-growing involvement in the purchase of businesses. Another community of professional contacts are accountants, lawyers, private banks and wealth management firms. There are over 50,000 in the UK alone. How many can you tap into?**

Most buyers do not read marketing material cover to cover, they will head for the financial summary and forecasts for the next two to three years. Make sure it's easily found. Acquirers will also want to see what the business does, why it's different from the competition and the reason for the sale. Avoid the temptation to have too much product/service information and detail. You are not selling your products or services, you are selling your business. This means you need to describe your business model, without jargon. Also, do not feel you have to answer every possible question in your marketing collateral. In fact, it is quite the reverse. You need to provide enough information for the potential buyer to want to meet you and ask the more detailed questions in person. It's like a first date: provide enough information to attract interest to meet. Avoid giving your life story, it's unlikely to help!

The most common thing missing in a marketing document is a financial projection for, say, the next three years. Business owners often say, "In my industry it's impossible to predict." "Poppycock," I say! Everyone can make a forecast based on your own experience and knowledge of the sector you sell into. If you can't forecast your own business financials, why would you expect a buyer to be able to? You must help a would-be buyer to see the possible shape and size of your business in the future. They need to understand how they are going to get a return on their investment and where the growth is going to come from. Marketing collateral that doesn't outline the future growth prospects simply gets shredded.

To avoid the dreaded shredding machine, use the tactic of:

phone - email – phone

Ring the prospective buyer and find out who is responsible for their mergers and acquisitions activity. Have a brief conversation with them and establish if there might be interest; if so, send a confidentiality agreement and then follow with your marketing document by email. Give them a few days and then make a follow up call. The purpose of that call is seek to book a meeting with them to talk through the detail of the business sale opportunity. I have found that it takes ten to twelve calls per prospect to get a decision whether to meet or not. People are often difficult to track down, always seeming to be in meetings or annual leave. You can expect to make at least 1,000 calls to prospects. If you haven't got the time and/or the confidence, find someone who does so that you can sell your business with the best marketing opportunities that will ensure that you earn its full value. The best marketing documents, often referred to as Information Memorandum (IM) contain the following:

- executive summary
- financial highlights
- operations overview
- opportunities for growth

Buyers assess future risk which will in turn affect the price they offer you. A compelling and well-written IM will help supply the relevant information and provide sufficient assurance that it would be worth meeting you to discuss further. Curiously, through the experience of contacting thousands of potential buyers over the years, we have noticed that a decline to meet one day can become an acceptance a few months later. The same person, same proposal they are looking at, but a different outcome. So getting a "no" today, isn't a "no" in the future. Catching people at the right time and keeping open the line of communication is crucial to generating meetings with potential buyers.

We've also noticed, especially in larger organisations, that one person in that company is interested and another not. Therefore, when selling your business, approach more than one person within a group structure. For example, contact the MD in the UK and also the CEO/President of the foreign parent company. They may well have a different appetite for a possible acquisition of your business.

CHAPTER 3

Commandment #3
"Don't just advertise your business, sell it"

The marketing collateral you use must be visually attractive and be informative whilst not giving all your commercial "secrets" away. It need only be twelve to fifteen pages in length maximum. Any longer and it will not be read. In my time I have come across numerous business sales prospectuses 80+ pages in length. They normally end up in the shredder. Nobody has time to wade through such monumental marketing material. Time is precious, especially for business leaders, and they do not spend it ploughing through another version of "War and Peace." Learn to be succinct and not to go into information to the "nth" degree. If your document is not read, you will not meet with buyers. The sole purpose of the marketing documents is to attract potential buyers to the discussion table. You should give enough information to help that happen, but no more. The "selling" of your business happens in person, round the table.

Like the selling of your own products or services, you need to understand what it is you have and what a buyer might find attractive, or not. Maybe have a trusted business friend critique your business in the form of strengths, weaknesses, opportunities and threats (SWOT). What are the current value drivers for your business and what new drivers are there potentially for the future?

> *Tip #3 – I would like you now to write down what you are selling. What is an acquirer receiving if they buy your business? Do not start off with "a long history, great reputation and excellent service." Think about the aspects of your business that make you unique or different. What are the "hidden assets" in your business – things that do not appear in your balance sheet, but nevertheless create value for your business? For example, a high repeat customer rate; expertise in a niche sector; low turnover of staff; and industry accreditations or awards. You should be able to come up with at least 20.*

The next step is to understand what acquirers are looking for, and conversely what they are not looking for. The following is a list of the top eight motives for purchase:

- acquisition of new client base into which to cross-sell and upsell
- future growth, especially in sectors with high barriers to entry
- geographic expansion, home and abroad
- securing newly developed products/services
- ownership of Intellectual Property, such as patents, design rights, copyright and trademarks
- benefitting from new operational and financial synergies
- attaining a new skilled workforce
- additional revenue and profitability

> *Tip #4 – How many of the above areas would be provided to the buyer, if they bought your business? More importantly, describe in what ways this could occur.*

16

A word here about confidentiality. All business owners are concerned about news getting out, but then some get carried away and do some inadvisable things. A few years ago I met a chap who proudly boasted that he had invented the successor to Facebook. He described how he had spent over three years writing the software platform and that Google had recently come over from the US to explore buying it from him. When I asked if he had got Google to sign a confidentiality agreement before he parted with commercial sensitive information and even a demo of the algorithms, he sheepishly said that he had not thought of it.

Always be mindful about information you disclose early in the process and always make sure the information given is under a strict "Non-Disclosure Agreement." It is advisable too to make sure you leave nothing in the office regarding the proposed sale of the business, nor indeed entries in your office diary that might lead your staff to query meetings.

Generally, my advice to sellers is not to share their plans for selling the business with anyone outside of the current shareholders. This is because there will be little to share with the staff and all it will serve to do is create uncertainty within your workforce and, worse still, leak out to your clients and suppliers. Normally it's far better to announce the sale when a deal is agreed with a particular buyer; then you can promote to the staff the benefits of being part of a larger organisation with greater career opportunities and a broader financial base.

Returning to "selling – not just advertising," make sure to view the purchase of your business from an acquirer's perspective. What is likely to be of interest to them? This needs to be amplified and focused on during discussions. Consider too, what is unlikely to be of interest to them? This needs to be left to one side and not be introduced in discussions. You would be surprised at how many sellers fall into the trap of telling an acquirer all about their business, including the parts that are not of interest or relevant to the buyer.

I had an arrangement with a client that I would pick up my pen in negotiation meetings when he was speaking too much or "off message." The type of character he was made it easy for him to waffle and to start unravelling the good work done earlier in the meeting. The pen worked extremely well as a prompt. When you are negotiating the sale of your business, make sure there are two of you. One to speak most of the time and one to primarily monitor things and make sure you keep on track with what you wish to communicate.

Selling is about establishing the needs or wants of the potential buyer and then focusing on how the purchase of your company could meet those same needs and wants. So the next question is, how do you find out what the buyer wants? The answer is simple, ask them. Enquire of them what they would do with your business, if they were to acquire it. Additionally, you can look on the internet and search for any press releases from them indicating their strategic plans for the future. Another possible source, especially with the much larger organisations, is to look at their chairman's summary on their annual company accounts. There can often be useful indications as to their acquisition growth plans. In reality, you are selling the future of your business under new ownership, and not its past under yours. Buyers can do nothing about the past. They can only influence the future and you ought to be helping the buyer see a clear picture about the future prospects of your business under their ownership. Your entire marketing and sales focus should reflect this. Focus on motives for purchase, not multiples of profit.

CHAPTER 4

Commandment #4
"Always decline a first offer"

In general, business sellers have never sold a business before. Conversely, acquirers usually have, many times. Often there is an imbalance of experience and skills. Professional negotiators never give their "best" price. Why would they? They are charged with buying a good business as cheaply as possible. After all, the quicker they get a return on investment post-acquisition, the better for them and their own shareholders, and the better they look to their board – and in some situations, the City. You must decline every first offer, no matter how tempting it might be, because there is always more to be gained. Here are some examples of actual deals I've been involved with in the past 12 months, showing what was offered initially and what their final position was after a period of negotiation:

Industry	Initial	Final
Construction	£1.5m	£2.41m
Telecoms	£4.5m	£5.92m
Environmental	£300k	£525k
IT Services	£850k	£1.31m
Tools & Equipment	£4.5m	£5.35m
Waste Recycling	£3m	£5.05m

There are some noteworthy points on this: it doesn't matter what industry sector you are in, this negotiating strategy is everywhere. Secondly, notice how the final sale price is a more precise figure, indicating that there is more science behind it compared with the opening bid. You will also spot how far apart the initial and final price positions are.

At this point, I should share with you that there is a considerable difference between the "price" of a business and the "value" of a business. The price of a business is typically calculated using a financial formula, often a multiple of profit. However, this is not the value of a business. The value of your business will vary from one buyer to another, depending on what it's "worth" to them.

Tip #5 – Never, never, never, give a price for your business to a buyer. Instead, invite indicative offers and be prepared to negotiate the price up with commercial and financial arguments.

The problem for you as the seller is that you do not know how much a buyer is prepared to pay to secure the ownership of your business. Why put a ceiling on that figure, by giving a hypothetical price? Conversely, if the selling price you have in mind is too fanciful and without a sense of some reality, buyers will simply walk away, not wanting to waste their time with a seller who quotes what they consider to be unrealistic price aspirations. As the seller, you need to establish the open market value of your business. This can only be done by approaching the market; speaking with real buyers, with real money. As with beauty, value is in the eye of the beholder.

Case Study 2

90-year-old family company sold to growing industrial group

For Anthony Record and his family, retirement was his goal for selling the company. Once Rob Goddard had completed his pre-sale study of the company, it did not seem to offer a huge potential growth proposition for an acquirer, at face value. Little potential can easily mean low offers – not a situation that any seller wants to experience. However, a combination of Rob's experience in mergers and acquisitions and the knowledge of the company and its markets he'd gained in the pre- sale period enabled Rob's team to identify several key areas that could deliver significant growth for an acquirer.

The Transaction

When Anthony Record, the CEO of Oswald Record Group, decided to sell the business his grandfather had founded in 1921, it was on the basis that a new owner would value what the company had achieved and enable it to achieve the growth he knew was its birth right. He instructed Rob to handle the sale, having evaluated two alternative brokerage services. Rob's approach to selling every business is firstly to understand the company, not purely from a financial perspective, but in terms of its business structure and strategies. The most successful sales result when the buyer and seller are both able to see the future of the business under new ownership so the ability to sell the potential is vital when marketing a business to prospective buyers.

Oswald Record was a well-established and well-managed company, commanding a 40% share of the UK Air Tools market and enjoying excellent customer loyalty, and thus repeat business. It had sole distribution agreements with leading manufacturers and an established position in the power tools market. With a nationwide sales and distribution network, it was a convenient, reliable supplier providing an excellent sales and after-sales service.

Brokering a sale requires commitment to customer service from the outset

Rob's assessment was that, with the adoption of new marketing strategies, extended product ranges and greater profit margin in the UK, there was true potential in the Oswald Record business. Applying strategic profiling techniques 70 potential buyers were identified and the marketing of the company began.

Five bidders submitted offers and the successful bidder was LSG Industrials, an investment company founded in 2010 as part of the LSG Holdings group with a mandate to invest in industrial and heavy plant businesses in the UK.

Anthony Record, welcomed the acquisition, commenting, "It was important for me to leave the business in suitable hands that would value what the company has achieved to date and allow the potential growth of the firm. LSGI's involvement will help the business achieve its goals to expand the Oswald Record's brand presence and operations across the UK."

For the team, this deal reinforced our belief that brokering a sale successfully is much more than a simple marketing exercise. It involves a commitment to customer service from the outset which is maintained right up to the point of completion.

This acquisition represented a strong synergistic/strategic fit for LSGI who went on to increase profitability and expand the customer base nationally, resulting in a net profit increase of over 300% in the 1st year post acquisition. Our client, retiring Managing Director Anthony Record, now enjoys a welcomed retirement, spending more time with his grandchildren, great grandchildren and his newly acquired renovation project, a 1936 Morris 8 Tourer!

Deal Summary:
    70 companies profiled and contacted
    5 potential acquirer meetings
    5 offers received

CHAPTER 5

Commandment #5
"Turn weaknesses into opportunities"

Mistakenly, sellers sometimes think they need to perfect their business before marketing it for sale. Wrong! The weaknesses of your business represent a great opportunity for a buyer and they are willing to pay you a premium for your business, to take advantage of the opportunity. I sold a business for what turned out to be a multiple of over 14 years adjusted net profit. This is largely because the buyer saw the huge opportunity of creating an on-line catalogue and centralising purchasing activity – something our client had neglected to do in four decades. With expected improvements in the year following acquisition, the buyer forecasted a trebling of net profit. So, for the buyer, they were seeing a multiple of profit of less than five.

> *Tip #6 – List all the weaknesses of your business and how a new owner might turn these into opportunities for growth. This list should form part of your negotiations, especially when buyers attempt to "chip" you on price later in the process.*

The ideal situation you want to achieve in the buyer's eyes is that you are doing everything "wrong," yet the business makes money year on year! Almost that your business is growing despite you. If you can take this place of humility it will help you achieve a premium price for your business. What you are in effect saying to a potential buyer is that "if you were to buy my business, with your greater infrastructure and resources, you could achieve far more than I have so far." Play to the buyer's ego. Why not? It's likely to be larger than yours!

The most common weakness I have found with Small to Medium Enterprises (SMEs) is that they lack a robust sales and marketing plan and approach. This is uncovered when asked the question, "How do you proactively secure new business?" The answer normally given is, "Well, we have a great reputation in the industry and so word of mouth is central."

A good answer, but it's to the wrong question. The key word I used was "proactively." What was described is a passive approach to sales and marketing, not a proactive one. Waiting for the phone to ring in order to gain new business is not a proactive approach to sales and marketing. In sales parlance this is called "order taking" not "order getting."

I once listed how many ways I could attract new business to my company – there were over 300 different activities. The fact that you may only currently use two or three routes to market is a weakness in your business model. However, to a prospective acquirer this represents an immense opportunity to drive the business forward, by making the business visible to a far greater pool of would-be customers or clients.

CHAPTER 6

Commandment #6
"Invite offers"

Your business is unique. You have unique individuals coming together and working under unique practices and systems. There is no business like yours. This is in stark contrast to selling a house, where there are likely to be other similar, comparables in your road or area, which can give an indicative price. Selling a business is not at all like that. The only exception are the public companies where their price per share is quoted on a stock exchange. In the world of the privately-owned business this doesn't apply. Forget about applying some arbitrary discount percentage of publicly quoted companies in your sector. It's meaningless. The value of your business will vary from buyer to buyer. They will value your business in accordance with what it's worth to them.

In my experience the range between the lowest and highest offers received on a particular business for sale can often be as much as 200% to 300%. Why? They have all looked at the same three year's statutory accounts, the same management accounts, and the same marketing material. Yet, the spread of offers is broad.

This is why you should never quote a price for your business. Statements such as "offers in excess of..." never work. All they serve to do is provide a ceiling value on your business. Buyers will see this as a cue from the seller that you are willing to consider an offer below this amount. Strange, but true. As the seller, you must set up a pool of competing buyers, who are encouraged to provide you with an indicative bid for your business. Naturally, their bid will be reviewed in association with others. Only then can you create competitive tension in order to help you increase price and improve exit terms.

It is worth mentioning that perceived competition is just as powerful as actual competition. I once sold a business in the engineering sector to BAE Systems. BAE asked at the first meeting if we were also speaking with Boeing. I replied that for reasons of confidentiality, I couldn't confirm one way or another. The reality was that Boeing weren't interested at all and declined to meet my client. BAE's initial bid was £1.1m, but after four months of negotiation they purchased my client for £3.2m. They were bidding against themselves and never knew it!

> *Tip #7 – Always decide on your "walk away" price as a Board of Directors, but never disclose it to buyers. Make this a price below which there is no point discussing further, but above which you would consider an offer further.*

A good friend of mine, George Swift, runs a mentoring business and one of his mantras is "double your prices!" The thinking is that people will pay well in excess of the market average for something if they believe it has value for them. The greatest number of meetings I have generated with buyers is fourteen, at which point my client said, "Stop finding interest, I'm sure we have found our buyer!"

CHAPTER 7

Commandment #7
"Appoint specialist advisers"

The largest bill you will pay on the sale of your business is likely to be to the HMRC. Behind that you will also need to pay a commercial lawyer to represent you. There are a multitude of law firms at your disposal in this country, but not all of them are experienced in selling business. Indeed, some of them actually get in the way of a deal happening. In my experience, there are good lawyers and there are bad ones. Good lawyers know the law, but are also pragmatic in getting the deal over the line. Bad ones know the law, but are more intent on "scoring" points against the other side. They lose sight of the ultimate aim – to sell the business. Deals can often be collapsed by this approach, with the seller not benefitting but still having to pay their lawyer's fees. Of course if your lawyer is on an hourly rate, it's not in his financial interest to take a pragmatic and expedient approach to a deal. The longer it drags on, the more he will be paid. It is better to insist on a fixed rate deal with a lawyer; that way you'll get the attention and focus you need. Good lawyers know which battles to lose in order to win the war. They are highly experienced with the complexities of Mergers & Acquisitions. It is not an adversarial environment that some lawyers are used to, it is consultative and collaborative interaction with the buyer's legal team.

Other fees to consider are your accountant's bill, if they have done additional financial work for you in preparation for the intended sale. You may also need to hire an M&A Broker to find buyers and negotiate a deal. Like most things in life, you get what you pay for. Do not be seduced by seemingly very low professional fees. Be sure of what you will be getting for the money you are paying. Is it value for money, rather than just being the cheapest? One area often neglected is the advice of an intellectual property expert. You may not think you have IP within the business. However, seek the advice of a specialist. Initial consultations ought to be free and you may discover something that you had taken for granted that could be protected, and by doing so could significantly enhance the value of your business to potential buyers.

> **Tip #8 – One way to ascertain if a lawyer is up to the specialist arena of M&A work is to ask them how many deals they successfully completed last year.**

One business I worked with had filed in 16 countries for a patent on their excellent invention. As part of what I was doing for them I also arranged for an intellectual property attorney to review what had been done. To his amazement my client had not filed for a patent in China … the world's largest market and fastest growing economy. It turned out that my client had inadvertently filed in Chile, not China! Selling a business is a team activity. It requires several professional advisers working together to achieve the desired outcome.

At one of my business owner Masterclasses a chap came up to me afterwards and said that he had sold his business in order to retire last year. He said that he had followed many of the principles that I had outlined himself and generated 20 potential buyers. I said, "That's great, and did you get the price you were looking for?" "Yes," he replied emphatically, "…but I haven't got the money." I was rather confused. He went on to explain that the final sale price for the business was for £500,000 and that his business was making around £100,000. A fair offer, given that there were only two other staff in his IT services business. However, there was no payment to him on completion of the sales transaction. Instead, all of it was spread over the following three years based on turnover targets being met. This is referred to as an "Earn Out." All of the value of the deal was structured around future performance. This is very high risk, because as soon as you sign your business over, you automatically lose control of the profit and loss potential. I was shocked and saddened to hear of the deal structure to which he had agreed. I asked him what he was going to do.

"I'm in the process of suing them. It's cost me so far £40k." I thought for a moment and replied, "You haven't sold your business, you've given it away, and if we had met a year ago, as your adviser I would have urged you not to accept. All the risk is on you; the buyer was not taking any risk whatsoever. It was a very bad deal for you. Why didn't your solicitor advise you against accepting it?" "Oh, I'm suing them too!" he declared.

Take expert/specialist advice in selling a business, it will save you money in the long run and help avoid disappointment and heartache. His planned retirement has been replaced by his having to pursue two legal cases which may cost him in excess £200,000 if it goes all the way to court. My advice to him would have been to keep the company, spend £40k of his annual profits in bringing in a managing director to run it, and that way he could take £60k dividends a year into retirement. Far better than giving it away on Day One. Get well-informed advice from people who handle business sale transactions for a living.

CHAPTER 8

Commandment #8
"Ensure that your claims match the paperwork"

It seems too obvious to even state this point, but many sellers fall into the trap of speaking about things that are not consistent with what is purported in the marketing material sent ahead of a meeting with a buyer. This understandably causes buyers to be distrustful of sellers, thinking, "Well, if this doesn't stack up, what else doesn't?" Do not contradict yourself or a fellow shareholder when in front of a potential buyer.

> **Tip #9 – Re-read the sales prospectus and any attached financial information just ahead of a negotiation meeting. You should know it inside out. Do not be tempted to "ad-lib" it.**

You do not need to be an expert, especially on financial matters. However, you will be expected to know the main numbers and an explanation of any significant historical trends. Be well informed on the running of your business, but avoid the danger of giving the impression that you are too knowledgeable. Buyers may draw the conclusion that the business can't run without you and this will be reflected in a lower price for your business.

Clearly, anything you say must be truthful, but you do not have to say everything. Knowing what to say and when to say it is a skill and not a science. You must disclose all relevant information, certainly where an indicative offer is made. In this way you can prevent a buyer trying to reduce their offer during the "Due Diligence" phase. You can legitimately say, "You knew of this information/situation before you made your offer and so we do not accept that there are grounds to reduce your original offer." Some business owners are usually tempted to waffle or talk at length. Avoid this at all costs. The more you talk, the more you are likely to say something unintended and possibly not consistent with what has been provided beforehand in the paperwork. Also avoid using expressions such as, "the trouble with this…" or "the risk with that is…" Using negative words will not fill a potential buyer with confidence about the future. Instead, they will have concerns regarding the future prospects of your business, which you inadvertently trigger into their thinking. Concentrate on using words with a positive connotation such as potential, growth and high demand. It sounds rudimentary, but many sellers forget the basics when in the heat of things with buyers.

A previous client of mine owned an audio and TV shop in the Midlands. When asked by a potential buyer why he was selling, my client's reply was "Well, to be honest, when the doorbell rings and another customer walks in, my heart sinks. It sinks because I know they are just coming in to ask for my technical advice on a piece of equipment, then walk out and go and buy it 30% cheaper online." Needless to say, this wasn't the reason given for sale in the prospectus we provided! Incidentally, honesty is not always the best policy … wisdom is the best policy. Clearly, everything we say needs to be truthful, but not all of the true, personal emotive reasons behind the sale need to be stated. In the case of my audio/visual shop client it is much better to say that the business was for sale because the current owner had taken it as far as he could after 30 years and that the business would benefit from new ownership in the next cycle of its growth. One potential growth direction would be to create an online catalogue and ordering system for customers across the UK and abroad. Prices could be competitively discounted on-line and we forecast a 30% increase in sale in year one. The current owner doesn't have the knowledge or skills to introduce this, but a new owner with the infrastructure and expertise could make this change. Additionally, the current shop, with its High Street presence could easily be developed into a centre of technical excellence. On-line for mainstream products, and in-store for the Hi-Fi specialist. Now doesn't that sound a better reason for selling? It's not what you say, it's the way that you say it.

CHAPTER 9

Commandment #9
"Be commercial, not emotional"

For most owners, selling their business is more of an emotional transaction than a financial one. This is especially so if you founded the business yourself and nurtured its growth through thick and thin to where it is now. It's your "child", and now you are selling it. So it makes utter sense to be very shrewd and careful about what terms and conditions you set when you let it go. If you don't believe me, wait until you start receiving low offers on your business from strangers who criticise and find fault with it. Then tell me you don't feel emotional about it! There have been times in my career where my client, the seller, has taken umbrage over what a potential buyer has said and this has resulted in them exiting the meeting in anger and frustration. I've even witnessed raised fists at times!

It is an emotive time, and this is a factor that most people are not prepared for when they sell their business. Emotions can often run high because the seller is personally attached to their business and the buyer is not. This may seem an obvious point; after all, to a buyer it is purely a commercial transaction. They have no personal history invested in the business, and this can be what gives them the advantage over you, the seller, if you are not aware of what you really feel about selling it. You may find that these feelings contradict all of the benefits that you look forward to in your life once the sale has been completed. Therefore, when negotiating a price, the seller must always go back to the buyer with a commercial argument as to why they should pay more and/or improve exit terms. This is the language the buyer will understand – and indeed expect – and will therefore more easily persuade them to go with your thinking.

> *Tip #10 – Create a three-year financial forecast that takes into account the financial and operational synergies and/or economies of scale derived from the two businesses merging. What happens to the turnover, costs and profit of the new, combined businesses? If you are not able to do this, find someone who can.*

An engineering business I sold a few years ago was barely making a profit. However, the eventual buyer was able to undertake some of the previously outsourced engineering processes, which put another £250k onto the bottom line and meant a further £1.3m on the sale price for my client. Be creative, look at it from the buyer's perspective. If you combined both businesses, what costs could you take out? More importantly, what cross selling and upselling opportunities could there be?

1 + 1 = 3, or even 4!

Also look for what new opportunities would be created from combining expertise, contacts and infrastructure. A buyer is not simply going to pay you more because you want more. You need to provide a sound commercial argument as to why they should increase the price they first offer.

CHAPTER 10

Commandment #10
"The devil is in the detail"

From experience, it is relatively straightforward to agrees, in principle, the main aspects of a potential deal. Where it can unravel all too quickly is in the detail behind what was meant. Make sure that the key agreements are confirmed in writing, and above all, be pragmatic. You can't have everything so be prepared to give a little in order to achieve an outcome that works for both of you.

> *Tip #11 – When you have decided which buyer to go with, ensure you draw up a detailed "Heads of Terms" document. This should clarify what exactly was intended and also what happens in certain situations. This document is signed by both parties and whilst not being legally enforceable, it does act as a point of reference by all if there is an issue further down the line.*

Never assume that your deal is straightforward or simple: it isn't. Buying and selling a business asset is fraught with risk for both parties. Pre-handle potentially difficult issues so that they don't cause the deal to falter. There is a golden rule in M&A: the longer a deal goes on for, the less likely it is to complete. We refer to it as "deal fatigue." People simply get tired of going round in circles, making little progress. Momentum in the sale process is essential to a successful outcome. So make sure you agree a workable timetable to act as a framework for the process to operate.

> ***Tip #12 – Always be prepared to trade something during negotiations that has high value to the buyer but is of low value to you.***

This will help ensure that the process moves forward in a collaborative and pragmatic way, for the benefit of both parties. After all, a successful deal is one where both parties believe they have "won." This is especially important if the current owner has the option of staying on post-sale.

CHAPTER 11

Commandment #11
"Be realistic about life after sale"

The most frequent reason for a deal collapsing is, in my experience, that the seller changes their mind. What I refer to as "seller's remorse." A friend of mine who studies the workings of the human mind calls it "post-decision regret." It's a feeling I had once when I signed a contract to buy a £50k Mercedes. I remember thinking as I left the dealership, "My God, what have I just done!? Should I try and cancel the contract I've just signed?" In the context of selling a business, 'seller's remorse" tends to emerge after approximately four to five months into a project, when offers are coming in and the whole thing is becoming very real to the seller. A negative view can set in – some clients I have worked with momentarily lost sight of the positive reasons for selling their businesses and began to feel anxious about making themselves jobless or redundant. It is important to keep in mind that there is bound to be an element of fear associated with making the leap from work to having more leisure time, but this does not mean that selling is the wrong decision.

Ultimately it's not about the money, it's about fear of losing a purpose and significance in life. Losing a reason to get up in the morning. Losing the environment whereby staff can seek your sage advice and wise counsel on issues. True, within a couple of months this will be gone so it is a good idea to plan constructively for what you will be satisfied to replace this role with. Uncertainty about the future is often linked to a perceived loss of identity. The ultimate result is that the seller has a knee-jerk reaction and takes their business off the market, instead deciding to continue to run it, with some vague thoughts about growing it further. I used to be a bank manager. Back in those days an unsettling statistic was that the average life expectancy in this profession was just two years following retirement. No wonder then that voluntary redundancy in banking was never fully embraced by its managers!

When considering selling your business, think very carefully about what life after sale will mean to you. What will you do? Will you move back to where you grew up? Move to a new country? What does life look like for you? Do not embark on selling your business until you have a basic plan as to what you will do after it is sold. It doesn't need to be mapped out in fine detail; just a sense of what the new chapter in your life will entail.

> *Tip #13 – Do nothing directly after your business is sold. Go on a long holiday to rest and reflect on the exciting future that lays ahead. Get used to choosing to work and not having to work.*

Over the years, many of my former clients have gone back into business in some shape or form. Few actually retire, finding that it is in their blood to be active in the business world, often investing in several businesses all of which benefit from their input and expertise. It's also possible that a potential buyer will offer for you to stay on under new ownership. Whilst this might seem appealing, think extremely carefully about this. When is the last time you had a boss? Think what it would be like to have someone you report to who can say "no." It takes a strong person to avoid thinking under new ownership, "it wasn't like that in my day." If you can stay on in the role of a steward who steers the company and provides it with stability while the new owner takes it in new directions, this might be a fabulous option.

Think carefully about exactly what stay-on role is being offered to you though, and how you will adjust to it.

Life after selling your business may well be very different. Cultural and operational changes, new initiatives introduced, and all at the behest of the new owner. Are you prepared to observe all these changes? My advice to most business owners is to make a clean break of things. Of course, by all means if it feels right, stay on in some form of part-time consultancy role, for an agreed handover period to ensure a smooth ownership transition. However, to remain as part of the management team post-acquisition is something to be considered very carefully.

It's often an impossible situation for the former business owner, particularly if some of the sale price is dependent on future performance, because you may lose out financially. A clean break is often best for all parties. (Please see Case Study 3 on page 42 PharmaQuest Ltd). Our client sold to the second highest bidder even though the offer was £1m less in the sale price. One simple reason: it represented the ability to walk away straight after completion of the deal.

Case Study 3

Specialist Translations Company sold to RWS Holdings

In the world of medicine, patients own assessments play an increasing and vital role in treatment and care development. The information gathered in Patient Recorded Outcomes (PROs) is multi-dimensional, assessing health related Quality of Life, Symptom Assessments, Patient Satisfaction etc. Patient Reported Outcome data is gathered through questionnaires that are constructed to measure and quantify the information gathered in a standardised way. Translating PROs is a complex task which follows a strict methodology in order to enable accurate assessment of data from multi-national trials.

Our client, PharmaQuest Limited, provided translation of PRO questionnaires to an international client base which includes pharmaceutical companies, clinical research organisations and academia. One of its shareholders co-authored the internationally recognised Principles of Good Practice for the Translation and Cultural Adaptation Process for Patient-Reported Outcomes Measures. The two major Shareholders, Darren Clayson and Aneese Verjee-Lorenz, established the Company in 2005. Both were qualified in Health Psychology and had considerable experience in outcomes research. PharmaQuest is unique in its field, combining the expertise of an outcomes research organisation with the credentials of a translation company and is, therefore, able to follow the entire lifecycle of a PRO project and provide an exceptionally high quality of service. The shareholders knew that in order to realise PharmaQuest's significant opportunities for national and international expansion, it would need to be part of a larger concern.

The Transaction

In 2012 the shareholders, therefore, made the decision to sell the business. After evaluating several potential business sales advisers, they appointed Rob and his team. Rob's approach to selling a business is firstly to understand the company not purely from a financial perspective, but through its business structure and strategies. By so doing, they are able to explore the potential of the company to a new owner, which in turn enables them to identify prospective acquirers which would have a "strategic fit". The most successful sales result when the buyer and seller are both able to see the future of the business under new ownership.

Within two months, the team had completed a detailed profiling of potential acquirers in the USA, the Far East and UK. When the project launched in October 2012 Rob's Business Development Team contacted 86 companies which resulted in 12 exploratory meetings with prospective acquirers. The team generated a number of offers from interested parties. One of the preferred offers was from world leading translation company, RWS Group, a well-established company that had extended its services into the Pharmaceutical/Medical Translations sector through a previous acquisition. They were seeking to grow that part of the business and their CEO could see that the synergies that would result from the acquisition would help RWS gain an even stronger foothold into the Medical Translations Sector. Our clients accepted the offer from RWS and the transaction completed on 30th April 2013, just six months after appointing us. RWS Executive Chairman Andrew Brode commented:

"We are pleased to have acquired PharmaQuest, whose progress we have monitored for several years. We look forward to growing PharmaQuest, with the benefit of the Group's infrastructure and marketing resources, and to broadening our market share in the medical and pharmaceutical industries".

Deal Summary:
86   companies profiled and contacted
12   potential acquirer meetings
2   offers received
Deal completed in 6 months

CHAPTER 12

"The 7 cardinal sins of selling a business"

If you want to do it all wrong, leave money on the negotiating table and sell your business for a *low* price, you just need to follow these rules:

1. Negotiate with only one potential buyer

2. Give a guide price for your business

3. Neglect the business during the sale process

4. Go back on your word with buyers

5. Have an inflexible mind

6. Not know the true value of your business

7. Not prepare your business before marketing it

According to a recent survey, only 7% of UK companies marketed for sale, actually sold. That's right, a 93% failure rate! *(Source: Coutts & Co. Bank "The Myths of Selling a Business")*

It's easier to be "sinful" than to do the right thing.

CHAPTER 13

"Revelations"

My experience in the industry of selling businesses has led me to the following conclusions:

Firstly, the process of selling a business rarely goes the way one envisages, but as long as there is a framework for the process and you appoint the right team to look after your interests it should help you smooth out what is often a "rollercoaster ride."

Secondly, the need to sell is greater than the need to buy. Look upon buyers for your business in the same way you look upon your own customers or clients. You want them to part with money. Do not be inflexible in your diary or late for appointments with buyers. Certainly do not take annual leave during crucial times of the sale process. This frustrates buyers and erodes goodwill. It also sends out the message that you are not committed to the process.

Following the principles outlined in this book should help you to navigate the often turbulent waters of selling a business. It's worth the effort and the benefits can be seen on the following page.

Business sold	Profit Before Tax	Sale Price	Multiple
Construction Equipment	£170,000	£2,400,000	14.1
Environmental	£83,000	£525,000	6.3
IT Services	£432,000	£5,100,000	11.8
Manufacturing Services	£948,000	£8,700,000	9.2
Financial Services	£872,000	£7,800,000	8.9
Recruitment/Training	£1,730,000	£14,300,000	8.3
Recruitment	£222,000	£1,000,000	4.5
Healthcare	£637,000	£4,200,000	6.6
Translation/Linguistics	£490,000	£3,000,000	6.1
Waste/Recycling	£547,000	£5,000,000	9.1

An interesting observation about the table is that two companies sold were involved in the same industry sector, recruitment. However, there was a wide variance in the multiple achieved. The same sector, but one was far greater in size and also benefited from an additional division of training. Larger companies with a broader range of services tend to attract higher multiples from buyers. Also, regardless of what industry sector you are involved with, the principles contained in this book apply. They are completely transferable across all sectors. There are as many deal structures as there are deals. It's not just about the headline price, it is about how payment will be made to you and in what format(s). You will recall the example earlier in this book of the chap who had effectively given his business away, because 100% of the sale price was going to be paid based on future performance.

"Earn-Out" deal structures are not in their nature "bad." It's the figures that fit into them that count. By this I mean that if the amount paid to you on completion was what you were looking for, any future payments in the deal would be "icing on the cake." Another common deal structure is "deferred payment." This is a mechanism whereby you do not receive all of the sale proceeds on Day 1, but there is a timetable for payment. The difference here is that payment of the future instalments is not dependant on future performance. They are guaranteed via such things as an "escrow account," personal guarantee or some other form of security. However, bear in mind that having a contract and security is one thing, but enforcing it is another and could turn out to be costly in legal fees if you needed to take such action. Take care if the amount you are being offered for your business is not all paid on completion. If the deal structure isn't acceptable to you, be prepared to walk away.

A quick word on something that afflicts most of us as business owners is the "tyranny of the urgent." Most business owners never get round to the important things in the business that are not urgent, for example business planning or long term goal setting. If that is you, would you like a simple strategy that will increase your productivity by 50% overnight?

Tip #14 – Never open your email inbox until 4pm

Emails, just like a ringing phone, are an interruption. They mean that someone is putting their agenda for the day ahead of yours. They distract you from what you need to achieve that day. Resist the temptation to look at your emails as soon as you've woken up. They can wait until the afternoon. Instead, plan what you need to do, who you need to contact, who you need to email. You set the agenda for the day, not others. Take control of the priorities in your life. Thank you to Lee Allan who passed that pearl of wisdom to me. Keep close to the best practices outlined in this book and you can be sure that you are selling your business for all it's worth. Whatever your plans for after you sell, I wish you a long, fruitful and happy life.

CHAPTER 14

"Apocryphal Writings"

This following section contains the saga and wise counsel from people I admire and respect, with whom I've had the pleasure of working over the years. One person doesn't have the complete answer, it's the blend of opinion and views that help you make the right choices and decisions in your business. Selling a business is a team activity. It requires a broad range of skills, expertise and insight to achieve a successful outcome.

Preparing for Due Diligence When Selling Your Company

Shareholders thinking of selling their companies will be familiar with the term "due diligence" but few perhaps realise how extensive and tortuous the process often becomes.

Once the initial terms are agreed, your buyer will wish to review the commercial aspects of your business, such as contracts, staff and key customers, so as to ensure the claims you have made about the business are accurate – this is the due diligence process. Once you have agreed the price and other heads of terms with the buyer, the investigation process commences, often in parallel with the legal process. Whilst your company lawyers are necessarily involved in both processes, time and money can be saved if you are able to anticipate the questions which will be asked during due diligence – the process is likely to cover:

- historic and forecast financial performance
- accounts
- asset valuation
- legal and tax compliance
- legal action against the company
- major customer contracts
- intellectual property protection and licensing
- employment issues

Your buyer and their advisers are likely to spend some time at your premises reviewing original documentation but the process will need to be controlled by you to guard against possible theft of commercially sensitive information and it being used as an excuse to renegotiate the deal.

As the due diligence process nears its conclusion, you and your advisers should finalise the sale agreement. This will contain exact details of the sale. There is likely to have been a measure of compromise on both sides to achieve a final sale document, but where you compromise you should ensure, against professional advice, that there are no surprises about future liabilities through the working of sellers' warranties and indemnities.

For assistance and support during the sale process it is essential that specialist legal and tax advice is obtained.

Matthew Cook
Bright Solicitors LLP
www.brightllp.co.uk

Earn-Outs on the Sale of a Business

It is not unusual, particularly in the current economic climate, for a buyer to wish to postpone or defer the payment of some of the purchase price when buying the shares or assets of a company.

One way to defer payment of some of the purchase price is with the use of what is usually known as an earn-out structure. This is where part of the purchase price is calculated by reference to the performance of the business being bought for a fixed period of time after completion of the purchase. The classic earn-out is calculated by reference to profits (although earn-outs can be linked to alternative financial measures).

Where the suggestion of an earn-out structure is based on sound commercial reasoning (e.g. not just because the buyer is going to struggle to raise sufficient funds in time for the proposed completion date) they can be beneficial for a seller as they may allow a seller to reap the full benefit of a profitable business. However, there are a number of things that a seller should consider before agreeing to an earn-out structure.

If you are considering accepting an offer where an earn-out structure is proposed, you should be aware that there may be some conflict between your own interests and those of the buyer. You are likely to have a short term view, wanting the immediate profits of the business to be as high as possible, whereas a buyer may want to make changes or invest in the business in a manner which may reduce the initial profits but be conducive to higher long term profits.

In view of potential conflicts between seller and buyer earn-out protection provisions will be very important to a seller in order to ensure that the deferred amount of the purchase price is protected and, of course, as high as possible. Issues you might want to give some thought to include restrictions on the buyer during the earn-out period e.g. not to sell off material assets of the company or wind the company up, an obligation on the buyer not to divert business away from the company, and general goodwill obligations. Your solicitor should advise you on all of the relevant issues. The protection provisions in the purchase agreement are likely to be the subject of much negotiation. Obviously, the larger the part of the purchase price that is represented by the earn-out, the harder you will want to negotiate.

Whilst a seller does not have to remain with the business where earn-out provisions are included, it is usual for them to do so (not least to try and protect their earn-out!) and therefore if you are a seller looking to retire or pursue other ventures then an earn-out structure may not be appropriate for you.

If you are going to remain with the company during the earn-out period (or beyond) you will also want to consider the terms of your employment or consultancy, and how the earn-out will be affected in the event that such employment or consultancy is terminated.

Another thing to consider with an earn-out structure, as with any structure where some of the consideration is deferred, is whether you will require security for the deferred part of the consideration. Security could include a personal guarantee or a charge over assets or shares and may assist you in the event of non-payment by the buyer, although be warned that requests for security are often met with some resistance from the buyer.

Finally, the way in which you structure any sale could have an effect on how much tax you will pay and as well as legal advice on properly structuring any earn-out and ensuring that the necessary protection provisions are included in the legal documentation, you should seek an accountant's advice on potential tax repercussions.

Peter Turner
Clarke & Son LLP
www.clarkeandson.co.uk

Selling Your Business: Picking the Right Legal Team

Do you know how you will choose your legal team when it comes to selling your business?

If you haven't had to deal with lawyers too often over the course of the life of your business, you may well assume that there is nothing much to distinguish one firm of solicitors from another and that any firm of solicitors should be able to handle the sale on your behalf. In fact, choosing the wrong firm of solicitors can, at worst, jeopardise the chances of your transaction closing or it could lead to difficult negotiations, delays and your assuming unnecessary levels of risk. The legal work associated with sales of shares and business assets is highly specialist. Our recommendation would always be that you should start by choosing a firm of solicitors who can demonstrate to you that they have a track record of successful deals behind them. The chances are that a buyer of a reasonably substantial business is going to appoint its own specialist team of advisers and it will soon become very apparent if your own advice is not of the same quality or that your team is unable to deliver their services within the same timescales as the other side. Your lawyers should therefore be able to resource the provision to you of legal advice (most likely across a number of different specialist areas in order to get the deal done) without keeping you and your buyer waiting and, if necessary, outside of normal working hours so that you can carry on running your business to the fullest extent.

By way of insight from the other side, we were involved in a transaction that very nearly collapsed a couple of years ago principally because the vendors had chosen to retain the services of a small non-specialist firm of solicitors who simply did not have the resources to cope with the various competing demands of a fast-moving and sophisticated acquirer – as our client in that case was. Not only was the vendors' solicitor trying to deal with various due diligence issues but he was also required to review, report on and involve himself in the negotiation of a detailed sale and purchase agreement and, at the same time, to manage his clients' disclosure process – an almost impossible task and a source of great frustration on our side. At one point we even had to lend secretarial support to the vendors so that they could get documents processed late at night when their solicitor's offices were closed!

Happily, we were able to push the deal through (notwithstanding) and the acquisition has been a success for both parties – it was, however, definitely a close shave for the vendors and would have been a great shame for them to have lost the deal simply because they chose the wrong firm of advisers.

Boyes Turner has one of the largest teams of Corporate lawyers in the Thames Valley. Our dedicated team has vast experience in sales and acquisitions of businesses in most sectors – both nationally and internationally, for businesses large and small and for sums ranging from anything to hundreds of millions of pounds. All of our deal teams are led by partners who are among the most highly rated lawyers in the country and we pride ourselves on being both proactive and accessible to our clients. While we look to deliver City levels of expertise and service we do it in a way which our clients tell us they enjoy and at rates that you could not expect to find in the City.

Robert Rice
Boyes Turner LLP
www.boyesturner.com

Could your business be more secure?

Running a successful business means constantly meeting and overcoming challenges. It's highly rewarding for you and your co-directors/partners when things go well. But when something goes wrong, perhaps for reasons beyond your control, the financial security of you all, and of all your families, could be at risk. The death of a partner/co-director can threaten all that hard work. Let's look at the potential problems and more importantly, the solutions.

Protecting the future of your business, the partners/directors of a business are its driving force and the reason for its success. What would happen if one is no longer there? If those shares end up with someone you don't know and who doesn't know your business, how would you feel? This is precisely what does happen if arrangements have not been put in place. Their share of the business passes on either through inheritance or sale.

- What are the problems for the remaining partners or directors?
- Find the money to buy the deceased partner's share.
- Continue paying income to the family until that share is paid off (perhaps from already reduced profits).
- Learn to accept the widow(er) as your new partner, with all that entails.
- Consider winding up the business.
- Competitors taking advantage of the situation.

So we've seen it from the survivor's point of view. But what if you die? Where does your own family stand in this? They've inherited your share of the business, but they're unlikely to be able to take over your role.

Do they have your skills, knowledge and experience? And would the remaining partner(s) be prepared to accept them?

Protecting the financial future of your family, what are your family's options?

- Take a share of the profits – This may not amount to much

if the business is struggling because of your absence. For how long will your partners agree to this?

- Insist on winding up the business
- Receive a share of its value. If the real value has fallen, they could receive little or nothing.
- Sell your share. This relies on finding a buyer who's prepared to pay the right price and that can be a long and difficult process.

The real solution is... The Westwood Succession Plan™

A structured pre-planned legal framework which ensures the succession of your business and protection of your wealth now and for future generations of your family

The Westwood Succession Plan™ provides funds to the right people at the right time, enabling the continuing partners/directors to buy out the deceased director/partner's family using the most tax efficient structures and bloodline protection is given to all the families of the partners or directors.

The Benefits
- An agreed succession to the surviving partners/directors.
- Adequate capital just when it's needed.
- A clean break between the business and the deceased's family.
- The business can continue to trade in its own right.
- No need for the deceased family to become embroiled in the business.
- Your family receives a guaranteed settlement from the business you've built up.
- Financial security immediately and continuing on for future generations.
- Valuable tax advantages and complete confidentiality.

Lee Allan
(Formerly Westwood Trustees Ltd)
Now, Grosvenor Associates
www.grosvenorassociates.com

Have you the best possible protection for your business from your employees/ex-employees?

Imagine if one of your key/senior employees left to join a competitor or decided to set up his/her own business competing with yours? This individual may know your business inside out and may have good relationships with your clients, employees and suppliers. Unless the business is properly protected there is a significant risk that a departing employee may take clients, employees and supplier relationships with them causing considerable damage to the business. History tells us that this regularly occurs.

One client I acted for lost £2.5m of turnover through having little or no protection in place. You cannot prevent employees from leaving your business, however you can limit what those employees can do during the employment and after they leave to ensure your business is protected. Your employment contracts and internal policies are your business's primary line of defence against employees disclosing confidential information or poaching your clients, contacts and employees.

Tightly-drafted appropriate post-termination restrictions can prevent an exiting employee from immediately working in direct competition with your business, stealing or disclosing trade secrets or poaching your key clients, contacts and staff, all of which could cause immeasurable damage to your business. Many businesses use precedents obtained from others which seem to have restrictions in place. This can be dangerous as these restrictions need to be tailored to your business and the individual against whom the protection is sought. In addition, many employment contracts are old and have not been reviewed or adapted as an individual is promoted in a business. In order to ensure that any restrictions are enforceable they should be regularly reviewed to ensure they continue to be appropriate to the employee's role and your business and should be reviewed as each senior/key person is recruited.

It is not just exiting employees who can cause damage. It is also important to ensure current employees are properly restrained from leaking confidential information to third parties, being engaged in outside businesses, taking Intellectual Property and/or causing damage during their notice period. This can be done with the appropriate clauses in the employment contracts.

Finally, over the last few years there has been a barrage of developments and changes to employment law. These changes have affected the way in which employers are required to handle their internal practices, manage their employees and resolve disputes in the workplace. For example, some of the particularly important areas of change include the abolition of the default retirement age, anti-bribery legislation, atypical working and pensions. To help avoid potential liabilities for your business it vital to ensure your contracts and policies are compliant with current legislation and where possible best practice.

In conclusion, therefore ask yourself whether you have the best possible protection for your business and when was the last review of your employment contracts and policies? Are you confident that your policies and procedures are compliant with recent changes to employment legislation and is your business adequately protected from the risks posed by employees both during and after the end of the employment relationship? Putting these measures in place does not cost a lot but could cause your business considerable damage without them.

The Hine Legal team can undertake an audit of your contracts and policies for an agreed fixed fee. We will then provide a report and recommend where we think amendment or improvement is required.

For more information, please contact

Nick Hine
Hine Legal
www.hinelegal.com

Poor "People Issues" Reduce the Valuation

Selling the business is an exciting time for an owner. Generally, it's been on the mind for a year or more. A potential buyer has been found, they seem keen and due diligence is about to begin. Plans to use the profits for a leisurely retirement or investment into the next "big thing" have been thought of and have become almost a reality. The future looks bright!

Whenever I've been asked to advise a CEO that's considering a merger and acquisition of a business I always ask whether retaining parts of the existing team is vital to success. The reason I ask is because how the vendor behaves in the lead up to a sale can result in fifty percent of the workforce leaving within twelve months and the other fifty percent over the following two years. "If that would reduce the value of the purchase, consider negotiating down the price you are asked to pay" is my advice.

Often the reason for the surprising statistics is that whilst the owner is living in the future the remaining workforce is firmly in a past time frame. Secure in a job they know and like. So when told that the business is to be sold a mass of insecurities rise to the surface and result in some critical talent considering their future. CV's will be prepared and recruitment companies contacted.

Losing key talent is not the only problem. Poor communication is often an issue. Informing the workforce too early allows competitors and head-hunters to circle around like vultures for rich pickings. Informing the workforce too late can cause disruption because on hearing that the business is being sold employee engagement tends to fall and with it productivity.

There is an increasing understanding amongst those advising the purchaser that "people issues" play a significant role in a successful M&A. Successful purchasers are encouraged to look at and address people issues early on during the due diligence phase. Difficult cultural fit, potential loss of key employees, past turnover, increases in turnover, poor employee communication, poor employee relations, reduced worker engagement, severance costs and potential constructive dismissal exposure can reduce the eventual price offered for the business.

Having a robust people plan that includes communication strategies, people issues and talent retention is part of maximising the value when preparing your business for sale.

Stephen Harvard Davis is the Managing Partner of Assimilating Talent that specialises in integrating senior talent into a business and working with restructured teams to make them more profitable faster.

Stephen Harvard Davies
Assimilating Talent Ltd
www.assimilating-talent.com

Preventing Uncertainty in Business Sales
(or how to make your buyer happy!!)

'Uncertainty will cost you pound notes!!'

This should be a mantra for anyone selling their business. If a buyer is not completely clear about the risks involved in the business he is buying then he is more likely to ask for a deferment in payment of the money due to you or possibly even a reduction in the overall purchase price. Such tactics are becoming more prevalent in today's climate. However, all is not doom and gloom as a good business will always sell and a seller can turn their business into a good business by reducing the risks a buyer faces.

Reducing a buyer's perception of the risks involved comes from planning your exit. You must not be forced into a situation where you end up selling because you need to get out of a business. Any buyer who senses desperation will aim to get a better deal for himself. To prevent this happening you should do the following things:

Give your buyer certainty of income:

- All buyers want to know that what they are buying will make money long term;
- if contracts are not in writing a buyer will argue that it can't predict the future;
- review all written contracts and make sure they are up to scratch and tie your customers in on your terms;
- watch out for 'change of control' clauses that allow your customers the chance to renegotiate or end a contract on the sale of your business;
- make sure your terms and conditions of sale and or website conditions of sale are up to date with current legislation, for instance, data protection and cookie policies.

Get your advisory team right:

- Unless you're a serial seller of businesses you'll need guidance;
- don't rely on your local accountant who has done your accounts for the last 20 years or your lawyer who bought your house unless they also sell businesses regularly;
- do engage an expert or that cheap quote from your mate at the golf club will end up looking very expensive.

Do deal with problem situations:

- That difficult customer could cost you thousands;
- if you know of product problems or potential claims settle them well before you plan to sell and make sure your settlement is in writing and legally binding. If it isn't the buyer's lawyer will have a field day with asserting that there could be future claims against the company.

Make sure your key assets are secure and in good condition:

- A buyer will not risk buying something it could lose;
- if you have lots of plant and machinery make sure it is regularly maintained under a maintenance contract;
- if you lease key assets then:
  - make sure the terms of the lease contracts can't be challenged on the company sale;
  - make sure that you have always complied with the
  - terms of the lease;
  - make sure the lease isn't about to end.
- If you are very IT reliant make sure you have a water tight disaster recovery plan and that all your data is backed up;
- if you are focussed on a sector that is about ideas or innovation, make sure your intellectual property is protected and that it is in one place and that the Company clearly owns it. The buyer will be buying your brand and needs to know it has total ownership;

- make sure your employees can't claim ownership over anything they've developed and that there are proper restrictive covenants preventing them going elsewhere and damaging the company.

Make sure you have a happy and properly contracted workforce:

- Happy employees work harder and earn a buyer more money;
- make sure your employees' terms and conditions are in writing and up to date with all legal requirements; employees like the certainty a contract brings and a buyer will be happier if it can see what its obligations are in black and white;
- if there are any disputes, settle them;
- if there is a problematic employee that needs to be
- removed take the advice you need to get rid of him or her, particularly if they are senior enough to have a material effect on the business

Don't tie yourself into long term liabilities:

- Don't sign long term contracts that are commercially burdensome;
- if you're tied into a long-term deal that is starting to look expensive, bite the bullet take advice on the contract terms and negotiate a release.

Do make yourself redundant:

- A buyer will want run your company his way and not rely on you;
- put in place a management team and make sure they buy into the future of the business and are motivated. This can be done by share option or bonus structure and a buyer will be much happier if there is a well-functioning team he can rely on;

- if a buyer doesn't need you it's easier to argue that the cost of your salary/dividends should be added back into the profit multiple thus increasing the purchase price.

Do know where all your records and documents are:

- If you can't find that property lease or your company's statutory books a buyer will start to worry about how you've run your company;
- conduct an audit and make sure that you have the documents that show who owns what and that give your company security. In particular, make sure you have all property details including deeds and leases.

All of the above steps take time and should be looked at least 12 months prior to sale and ideally 24 months before sale. Ideally, you should get a third party to help you look at all the aspects mentioned above because what you believe are not problems your buyer may see differently and it is their perception that matters. If followed properly you will turn what can be a difficult sale process into a much happier experience for all involved and importantly an experience, which doesn't cost you money!

For more information, please contact us on:
reception@hcbsolicitors.com

Adrian Leonard
(Formerly, HCB Solicitors)
HW Business Law LLP
www.hwbusinesslaw.co.uk

Emotional Insurance

Classical finance theory makes little room for sentimentality when deploying wealth in the quest for returns. But the surprising reality is that the failure of economic theory, and subsequently the financial services industry, to address the importance of emotion in investing is one of the primary sources of poor advice to investors.

The industry's traditional approach has essentially been to hand over 'optimal' portfolios built on the assumption that the investor will be completely focussed on long-term financial objectives at all times: 'Here's your ideal portfolio; it's mathematically optimal for your level of long term risk tolerance, and financially efficient. Now it's your problem!' This places a huge practical and emotional burden on investors – making it their problem to actually implement the portfolios and then to manage them through the often quite dramatic ups and downs of the investing cycle.

In borrowing the glib assumption of complete rationality from the theorists, the industry has been washing its hands of responsibility for a large part of good investment decision making – not just knowing what to invest in, but also effectively acting on this knowledge and controlling one's normal human emotional responses along the way.

By ignoring the important role of emotions, traditional portfolio solutions end up making investors uncomfortable along the journey and that frequently leads to poor decision making and lower performance.

When we're stressed, we naturally take decisions that help us to get more comfortable:

- *we pay too much attention to the short-term*
- *we over-react to market movements*
- *we invest in local assets or ones we're familiar with and shun similar (or better) risks which are less familiar*

68

- *we buy when markets are doing well and sentiment is high, and sell when markets are low*
- *and we retain large portions of our wealth in cash, unused and unproductive.*

On average, all these behaviours drag down long run returns. Despite what theorists may tell us, however, none of these is necessarily 'irrational'. We do get something in return – we get to sleep at night! The truth is we need emotional comfort. But a sequence of comfortable short-term decisions doesn't often add up to optimal long run performance.

Many investors sold in despair at the bottom of the markets in late 2008 and early 2009. In one sense, this was perfectly reasonable: if you're stressed, anxious, or even terrified that markets will keep falling, selling out provides an instant sense of relief from knowing you won't lose any more. But this is short term emotional comfort purchased at enormous financial cost. Once you've left a turbulent market for emotional reasons, it's almost impossible to get back in again, no matter how good the logical case for it. You lock in the losses and miss the eventual rally.

So, how much should you pay for emotional comfort? Traditional finance says 'zero': emotion is to be controlled, not pandered to. But when we aim for perfection, betting against the obvious and powerful force of human fallibility, we often fail completely and pay a huge premium to eliminate our emotional turmoil.

One easy and natural way of purchasing emotional insurance is simply to take less risk. But this can also be very expensive. It reduces long term returns, sometimes dramatically. When offered a choice between the scary but mathematically perfect portfolio, and not investing at all, many choose the latter because it's more comfortable.

By not investing, a moderate risk investor in a globally diversified portfolio foregoes long-term returns (averaged over many years) of about 4%-5% per year – a large amount to pay to ease discomfort! Just as it's not rational to aim for an 'optimal' solution that you know is unattainable, particularly when the costs of failure are high, it's also not rational to not participate at all purely for reasons of emotional comfort.

The right approach is to accept the need to sleep at night, and then ask how this can be best achieved. Identify the aspects of investing that make you most nervous and find targeted ways of reducing this anxiety as cheaply as possible.

At Barclays we use our proprietary Financial Personality Assessment to assist with this. It measures six different dimensions of your emotional responses to investing: three related to different aspects of your risk attitudes; and three to your decision making style. We use this to guide the selection of solutions that focus on providing the specific emotional comfort that is most psychologically important to each individual investor. This may be achieved by keeping some reasonable portion of your wealth in cash for security. It may mean purchasing downside protection in the event of extreme market moves. Or it may mean sacrificing some long term upside to focus the portfolio on investments that feel more comfortable. But all of these mean you can invest your wealth productively for the long term, and get to sleep at night. Yes, some people need a little more emotional comfort than others – but no-one needs to pay 5% of their wealth per year to get a little rest. In investing, as with every in life, do not let the 'best' be the enemy of the 'good'.

Greg Davies PhD
Head of Behavioural & Quantitative Investment Philosophy
Barclays Bank plc
www.barclays.com

Are you making the Most of Inheritance Tax Relief?

Qualifying businesses can attract business property relief (BPR) at 100% for inheritance tax, but it cannot be taken for granted. It can apply to company shares, interests in partnerships and sole traders, but this article concentrates on some of the key traps and pitfalls for the unwary shareholder.

If a company's business is wholly or mainly one of making or holding investments (i.e. over 50%) no relief is due at all – it is an all or nothing test. The risk is that a company's activities change over time to include an investment activity so that the test can be failed without the shareholders even realising it. An example would be a property development company that increasingly retains developed property as investments for rental purposes.

Where a company owns "excepted assets", i.e. assets which have neither been used wholly or mainly for the purpose of the business throughout the whole of the previous 2 years nor are required at the time of the transfer for future use for those purposes, a proportion of the shares' value will not attract relief based on the value of those excepted assets.

A further key point in relation to BPR applies to premises owned personally by the shareholder of a company and used wholly or mainly in that company's business. On the face of it this looks like a business asset but in practice only half of its value will attract IHT relief, and then only if the company is controlled by the individual shareholder, perhaps with their spouse. This contrasts with 100% relief which might apply to the value of the shares themselves.

Similar rules to groups of companies, but with the added complication that the BPR conditions must be considered at both company and group levels.

Similar tests apply for Capital Gains Tax (CGT) Entrepreneurs' Relief and Gift Relief. In these cases, however, the hurdle is somewhat higher in that the company must be over 80% trading by reference to a number of factors. This discrepancy creates a further trap when planning a family's affairs.

The BPR and CGT limits will catch many shareholders out and need to be kept under regular review so that any appropriate action can be taken at an early stage.

Stephen Barratt
James Cowper Kreston
www.jamescowperkreston.co.uk

Intellectual Property:
Why Protect It?

All businesses own and use intellectual property. Whether you sell products or provide services, your intellectual property, and its protection, is likely to be critical to your success. Here are three reasons why.

Distinguishing your business from the competition

Intellectual property is often associated with new inventions. But it's more than just this. A company's brand, the technology it uses, the data that it owns and the licences that it holds to use intellectual property owned by others, are all valuable assets that contribute towards distinguishing your business from the competition.

If a competitor starts using a brand that creates confusion and diverts customers away from your business or reverse engineers the software that you have developed that is otherwise unique in the marketplace, this could be extremely damaging to your business.

It is therefore vitally important that companies consider their intellectual property and obtain early protection for their assets to ensure that, if any such events do occur, they are in the best possible position to deal with them quickly and cost-effectively.

Growing your business

As your business grows, you may find yourself becoming increasingly reliant on your business partners (such as your suppliers, distributors and franchisees) with whom you may need to share your intellectual property. Whilst your contracts with these business partners should provide you with some protection against the misuse or unauthorised use of your intellectual property by them during the term of the relevant contracts, that protection may fall away at the end of the life of the contract.

Registered rights (where available) will provide you with the ammunition that you may need to discourage your business partners from walking away with your intellectual property once your relationship with them comes to an end.

Preparing for sale

The state of a company's intellectual property portfolio will be high on the list of items to investigate for any potential buyer. This is because a serious and experienced buyer will be aware of the importance of a company's intellectual property, and the need to protect it. If any issues are uncovered by the potential buyer during the due diligence process, this will at best lead to a negotiation over the purchase price for the business, or at worse to the buyer walking away from the deal altogether.

Claims (actual, alleged or threatened) of intellectual property rights infringement made against the target business or company by a third party are likely to cause a potential buyer the most concern. Steps can be taken to minimise the risk of this happening before the relevant brand is adopted or invention put into use. However, if appropriate searches were not carried out at the outset, it is still never too late to carry out a professional IP audit in relation to your business. This may uncover issues, but it will at least give you the opportunity and time to deal with them before putting your business up for sale.

Eesheta Shah
(Formerly Nabarro LLP)
Now, Marriott Harrison LLP

Business Protection:
3 Steps to Effective Planning

Business owners and their advisors will be familiar with the concept of business protection planning when considering the impact that the death or serious illness of a business partner or shareholder might have on the continued success, profitability and long-term value of their business. It is important to note, however, that in order to be fully effective, business protection planning is a process where the client's financial and legal advisors must work together to produce the desired outcome.

The role of the financial advisor is to assess and put in place adequate business protection insurance. Insurance aims to provide the remaining business owners with tax efficient funding, which they can use to purchase the deceased business owner's shares or partnership interests. However, in most cases, where insurance is taken out on the lives of the business owners, individual policies must then be assigned into a specialist business protection trust. This ensures that the proceeds of the policies remain outside the estates of the business owners and sums are freely available to the survivors, if and when needed. The third step is ensuring there is an appropriate partnership/shareholders agreement in place. This governs the tax efficient transfer of business interests to the surviving owners.

Unless all three steps are carried out there is a risk that the proceeds of insurance policies may fall into the wrong hands and may even be taxed as forming part of the deceased's estate. In addition, unless an effective partnership/shareholders agreement is in place there may be insufficient rules to allow a transfer of the business. Worse still, in some cases rules may be in place which actually impact on the availability of Inheritance Tax Business Property Relief. This could potentially create an additional charge to tax on the deceased's estate (of as much as 40%), on the value of their business interests.

Imagine the fictional case of Peter and John. They have been in business together for many years, as directors and principle shareholders of a private limited company. Through their hard work, specialist skills and industry knowledge their business has grown steadily, employed more staff and produced healthy profits for them as the owners. Peter and John hope one day to be in a position to sell up and possibly even retire early.

Unfortunately, one morning Peter is killed on his way to work. This is of course devastating for Peter's family, friends and for his business partner, John. From a business perspective John has lost a valuable partner, who contributed equally to the running of the business. It is doubtful whether John will be able to continue to generate the same level of turnover without Peter's future input. Peter's family has lost a husband, father and the main bread-winner. Under the terms of Peter's Will, his widow now owns the shares in her late husband's company, which may continue to provide her with some income. However, Peter's wife lacks the knowledge and skills to simply step into her late husband's shoes and, in any event, she must continue to care for the children.

John has not only lost his original business partner, but he now has a new business partner who is unable to contribute to the continued success of the business, but who will still be entitled to receive a share of the profits. John may, therefore, be faced with the prospect of setting up a new business on his own, leaving Peter's widow with shares in a worthless company. Both parties are left in a worst position. The situation would have been no better for Peter and John if, instead of dying, Peter had been left permanently disabled or diagnosed with a terminal illness. In that case, Peter would still be entitled to draw an income from the business, but again in the long-term John would have little motivation towards its continued success. Sadly, things might have been very different if only Peter and John had put in place an appropriate business protection strategy.

Had Peter and John undertaken business protection planning, insurance policies would have been taken out on their respective lives. The benefit of those policies should have been assigned into specialist business protection trusts. Failure to carry out this important second stage could see the policy proceeds falling into Peter's estate, being unavailable to John, as was originally intended. Assuming Peter and John did assign the policies into trust, the third step is ensuring there is an appropriate, tax efficient shareholders agreement in place, governing the transfer of shares from Peter's estate to John.

Assuming all three stages of the business protection planning had been completed, on Peter's death the business protection trust would have received a sum of money (tax free) equal to the value of his shares in the company. The shareholders' agreement would govern the transfer of shares from Peter's widow to John, but would be suitably drafted to avoid any loss of the valuable Inheritance Tax Business Property Relief on Peter's shares. The business protection trust could pay out a lump sum to John, which he can use to purchase Peter's shares. John is then free to continue to run the company on his own, or take on additional assistance if required and retain the profits. Peter's widow has a cash fund, which she can now invest to produce an income for her family. A bit of forward planning, therefore, acts in the interests of both the business owners and their families.

With all the immediate everyday pressures involved in running a business it is hardly surprising that little attention is paid to what would happen if a partner or shareholder died or became seriously ill. Nevertheless, it is certainly in the interests of every partnership or private limited company to do so if they wish to ensure the long-term financial security, stability and continuity of their business. Where business owners undertake such planning it's vital that financial and legal advisors work together to ensure all three steps are completed in the planning process.

Nicola Plant
Pemberton Greenish LLP
www.pglaw.co.uk

Intellectual Property Issues On a Sale

The importance of intellectual property in a share or asset sale will depend on the nature of the business that the company is engaged in. However, all businesses will to a certain degree either own or use IP under licence. If ownership or valid use of IP cannot be proved this will be of concern to a buyer, who may ask to pay less or/and require protection from the seller. It is therefore essential that consideration is given to IP and how to deal with IP throughout the sale process.

DUE DILIGENCE

As part of the sale process the buyer will carry out due diligence to determine:

- what IP does the business use or require in order to carry on its business?
- is that IP either owned by the company or licensed to it?
- if the IP is licenced, what are the terms of the licence?
- what proof does the company have that it either owns full title to or has a licence to use the IP in the manner that it is currently used?
- to what countries does the IP apply and is this geographic coverage sufficient for the business;
- what rights has the company granted to others to use the IP?

In respect of IP that is subject to registration due diligence is straightforward as either the IP is registered in the company's name or it is not. Some registered IP can be revoked on application by third parties and so the due diligence in respect of core technology may extend to a consideration of similar technology.

In the case of IP that is not subject to registration, ownership issues can be more complicated. For instance, if the material in which the IP exists has been developed by a third party the IP may belong to the third party.

78

When the third party was engaged it would be usual for the contract of engagement to have included an obligation on the third party to transfer all IP to the company. If such an obligation exists, it should be enforced. If none exists, then steps must be taken to procure that title in the IP is assigned to the company.

Where the company uses the IP pursuant to a licence the terms of the licence should be considered to determine:

- whether in the case of an asset sale the licence is assignable to the buyer and if so on what terms?

- whether on a share sale there are any change of control provisions that could lead to termination of the licence;

- whether the rights granted by the licence are sufficient for the buyer's future plans for the business.

With a group of companies IP may be registered in the name of a single group company with licences being granted to other group members to use that IP. In that case the seller will have to determine what IP is to be transferred or licenced to the target company on a share sale or to the buyer on an asset sale and the terms of such transfer and licence.

ASSIGNMENT OF IP

Once questions of the existence, ownership and assignability of IP owned or licenced to the business have been answered both the seller and the buyer must evaluate the IP. Matters to consider include:

- are there any unregistered IP such as trademarks which should be given the protection afforded by being registered in all relevant markets?

- if there is any doubt about the company's ownership of any IP (because for instance the material was developed by a third party) how is that issue to be resolved?

- is the geographic protection given by the existing IP sufficient?

- if important technology is inadequately protected by patents, is confidential know how about the technology held by employees and, if so what steps need to be taken to protect that know how?

- if licences of business critical IP could be terminated on a change of control or there is a possibility that they may not be assigned what alternative IP is available?

WARRANTIES

The nature of the warranties that will be required in respect of IP will depend on the importance of IP to the business and what has been discovered during due diligence. The following are likely to be required:

- that the company has all material or relevant IP required by the business;

- that all IP owned by or licenses granted to or by the company have been disclosed;

- that the IP owned or licenced to the company does not infringe any third party rights;

- that no third party is infringing IP owned by the company;

- that all registered IP continues in force, all fees have been paid, all necessary filings have been made and the registrations are not open to challenge.

In addition to the warranties it is likely that separate warranties will be sought in respect of computer software as part of warranties relating to information technology used by the Company.

CONCLUSION

IP can be a very important asset of a business greatly adding to its value. A lack of IP protection for core assets or products or a failure to maintain and enforce IP belonging to a business can reduce the value of a business and endanger its survival. For these reasons proper due diligence and evaluation of IP should always be carried out as part of a sale by specialist IP lawyers followed by careful consideration of how to deal with matters raised in that process.

Ian Brent
(Formerly DAC Beachcroft LLP)
Now Fladgate LLP
www.fladgate.com

If Your Business Lost a Shareholding Director, Would It Survive?

Your company is probably working harder than ever. The experience and expertise of the directors at the top of your organisation will be crucial in steering it through what may be the toughest trading period in its history.

But what happens if one of those directors, who is also a shareholder in your business, dies or becomes critically ill?

Of course you'd miss their presence, as well as their experience and expertise. But do you know what would happen to their shares?

An uncertain future

The dispersal of a director's shares could have a significant impact on your business's stability. The shares might pass to another individual who has little knowledge or interest in the business.

They may even gain significant control of the company and take decisions that may not be in the best interests of the other directors, employees or customers.

You could always make arrangements to buy those shares back, but could the remaining directors afford to do so?

Mitigate the risk

Depending on your circumstances and the structure of the business, there are a number of ways to ensure that the business can continue to run.

One solution is to insure against the loss of key personnel. It could be that a shareholding director becomes incapacitated and cannot make decisions for the business.

Succession planning is a good idea to make sure there is someone to step in if required. This could be a team member who is groomed for the role.

There are interim managers who can step in and help a business at this difficult time.

All these may well require additional, unforeseen, funds.

Howard Schaverien
Capital Solutions Ltd
www.capital-solutions.org.uk

Parents Beware!!! The Liability of a Corporate Seller for Claims Against Its Subsidiary

The Court of Appeal decision in Chandler V Cape plc [2012] has important implications for those involved in corporate disposals and legal due diligence. In this case the Court found that a parent company can owe a duty of care to an employee of a subsidiary. The claimant, Mr Chandler, had been an employee of Cape Building Products Limited (CPBL). During the course of his employment he was exposed to asbestos and later developed asbestosis. By the time of diagnosis CBPL had been dissolved and Mr Chandler therefore commenced proceedings against the parent company, Cape plc, and ultimately succeeded in claiming an award of damages.

The decision stands in contrast with the long established principle that the acts and liabilities of a company are its own and not its shareholders. The Court of Appeal in Chandler found that a parent company could be liable if it can be established that the parent owed a duty of care to the claimant.

The Court found that a duty of care existed between the parent and the subsidiary's employee because:

1. The business of the parent and subsidiary were the same in the relevant respect;

2. The parent had (or ought to have had) superior knowledge on some relevant aspect of the health and safety in the particular industry.

3. The parent company knew (or ought to have known) that the subsidiary's system of work was unsafe; and

4. The parent knew (or ought to have foreseen) that the subsidiary or its employees would rely in it using that superior knowledge for the employees' protection.

From the conditions outlined above it is clear that the decision came short of replacing the principle that that the acts and liabilities of a company are its own and not its shareholders but did provide an alternative solution to attach liability to the parent company.

The judgment will raise concerns for any parent company relying on a group structure to protect itself from claims brought against a subsidiary. The Court examined the nature of the relationship between the parent and its subsidiary. Parent companies should therefore consider how they interact with their subsidiaries and whether such interaction could be construed in such a way that it could lead to the establishment of a duty of care.

In summary, the disposal of a subsidiary will not necessarily relieve the corporate seller from a duty of care which may exist. Buyers should ensure that, if it appears that a duty of care could exist, the apportionment of any liability is properly set out in the transaction documents. A buyer's due diligence enquiries should focus on the relationship between the companies within a group structure and, in particular, the control exerted by a parent over its subsidiaries. Whilst this decision concerns a duty of care in relation to breaches of health and safety responsibilities the principles set out in the Court judgment may also be applied to other areas, in particular environmental breaches.

David Few
Blandy & Blandy LLP
www.blandy.co.uk

Building value for the sale of your company

1. Build the niche

A focused niche player will attract buyers because it is likely to have strong margins, be more profitable, and have greater barriers to competitive entry.

A+ companies have overall profitability in the range of 18%-plus, as a percentage of sales, and sometimes go as high as 25% or 30%. They are often dominant players in their particular focused market, and they usually offer some products no one else does.

They typically have a defined business category that they understand well, and this enables them to be first with changing technologies and trends in their segment.

2. Build a financial track record

Buyers look for strong profitability, steady progress over recent time periods, and solidity of fundamental balance sheet. The more you can keep costs well controlled and profits growing, the better.

As you build, your plans should include steady and fairly aggressive pay-down of debt. The truly healthy company, with minimal debt and/or strong cash, is highly reassuring to buyers, and generates strong confidence quickly.

3. Understand growth potential

Even the best niche market in the world, if its total potential size is tiny, is not very attractive. Measure the size of your primary customer segment today and its predicted size taking into account future growth.

As you begin to see weaknesses in the market road ahead, look for possible replacement segments in emerging new markets.

Analyse demographic and retail trends, and every other bit of information you can glean, to give you glimpses of the possible future.

4. Secure the intangibles

Intangible assets enhance value. The most obvious intangibles are:

- patented products

- products subject to exclusive supply agreements

- trade names and trademarks.

Be diligent about the legal maintenance of such intangibles. An equally important – but often neglected – intangible asset is key people. A firm, long-lasting non-compete agreement for top management should be in place well before you start to think about selling.

5. Do your housekeeping

"Housekeeping" means:

- maintaining clean financial records, with annual audits or reviews by an outside accountancy firm

- having defensible tax positions – nothing outrageously risky or "on the edge"

- having clean environmental and safety records

- complying with governmental rules and regulations

- fully and properly adhering to rules for taxes.

In addition, any buyer paying an aggressive price will expect the seller to make certain representations and warranties about the condition of the company being sold, and to say that he has fairly disclosed known threats and claims. He will also have to attest that he has told the truth and has not misled the buyer intentionally.

Positioning for the future

You can build into your plans the mechanisms to enhance the value of your company. By doing so, you ensure that your company will be worth more in the future, and you increase its stability and security right now. You make your employees safer, in that they will be more desirable to a future buyer of the premium company. The outcome can be the best possible for everyone.

Terry Irwin
TCii Ltd
www.tcii.co.uk

Protect Your Business Against Your Customers' Financial Difficulties

In the current economic climate, many businesses are struggling to meet their payment obligations in time, which often has a direct negative impact on a supplier's cash flow. Here are a few tips to help protect your business:

1. Do your research! Undertake Companies House and credit searches against new customers. Remember that your customers' circumstances can change over time, so make sure you update these searches regularly.

2. Secure debts! Seek a guarantee from the directors or the parent company if there is concern over any new customer. If a company becomes insolvent, secured creditors are first in line to receive what they are owed.

3. Insure! Taking out credit insurance can protect your business against insolvency or non-payment of invoices.

4. Review your terms! Ensure that your commercial contracts / terms and conditions / invoices state the payment terms very clearly: When is the amount is due? Who is it payable to? How is it to be paid? Make sure your terms and conditions are properly incorporated in all your contracts and include a retention of title provision which allows you to retain ownership of your goods until your customer makes full payment.

5. Ask for advance payment! Do not hesitate to ask for money on account / payment upfront / a deposit.

6. Clarify your payment due date! Make it clear that payment is due on presentation of a bill and give your customers no more than 30 days to effect that payment.

7. Incentivise! Consider offering a financial incentive for early payment.

8. Invoice regularly! If you are likely to be involved on a lengthy project, invoice your customers periodically for smaller amounts rather than for the whole amount at the end of the project. This will help with your cash flow and will also enable your customers to know what to expect and stay on top of their financial commitments.

9. Keep yourself informed! Talk to your customers regularly in order to be able to anticipate late payments and protect your own cash flow. Know when to adopt a conciliatory approach to late payments in order to retain a customer who may just be going through temporary challenging times and when to adopt a stricter approach to repetitive late payments.

10. Prioritise debt collection! Put a robust credit control system in place and put debt collection at the top of your to-do list. Decide when and how customers will be chased for late payment and when a final demand will be made. Make sure you retain written evidence of your communication exchanges.

11. Know your termination rights! Check your rights to terminate your commercial contracts, if the customer becomes insolvent or fails to pay.

12. Take action! Unless you decide to write off a debt as a bad debt to save on cost and time, consider instructing a bailiff or issuing a winding up / bankruptcy petition.

Bryan Bletso
(Formerly Pritchard Englefield LLP)
Now Irwin Mitchell LLP
www.irwinmitchell.com

Why exiting your business should be at the beginning of your business strategy!

Do you intend to exit your business? When?

When I'm talking to business owners and ask these questions, very rarely do I get more than a couple of people putting up their hands. Then I make the very bold statement that every single person will exit their business whether they like it or not; we will all exit our business. The only question is whether we do so in a coffin or in a taxi to the airport. The time to plan for that is now, whilst you have the time to influence the future that you want, and the legacy you want to leave. Wherever you start, you should always do so with the end in mind.

In my experience, I would say that the majority of business owners started their business in order to provide a certain amount of finance and safety and security and abundance for their family. Ironically though, if they do not put the right systems in place, the very vehicle that they are setting up, to create the freedom that they want for their family could be the very vehicle that leaves their family impoverished when they go.

If you do not have the right succession plans or the right exit plans in place on your business, and you do happen to die, then you leave a very, very big problem for the family left behind. The problem may be so complex that it probably won't be unravelled. As a result, the business would collapse and may even leave your family with debts and problems in your wake. That's just from poor planning, and poor strategy. That is why this stuff is so important.

So, when we're looking at the long term strategy, it is really important to have your preferred exit scenario clearly in mind and to picture what that looks like, and you have a number of choices.

For example, one solution is indeed to sell. You build a company over three to five years with a clear plan to exit, sell on to somebody else and then probably set up another one. That's very much the mark of a serial entrepreneur.

For many SMEs, the mindset would be different. For them, it is a lifestyle business and built around their passions and what they really enjoy. They are in this for life and so need to have a different strategy in place, such as the exit of self or removal of self over time.

This means just putting in and layering in the right senior management team within the company so that, maybe within three to five years, you can exit yourself and leave the company in good hands. You would still own the company and maybe act as chair person or chairman or even as a non-executive director, but the company effectively runs itself and you just reap the dividends.

The important thing is that you have the choice of having some active involvement if you wish, but it's entirely up to you. Giving yourself choices is the key thing in exit.

Deri Llewellyn-Davies
Business Growth International Ltd
www.bgistrategy.com

The Legal difference between a share purchase and an asset purchase

One of the biggest decisions for a seller or purchaser of a business is whether to opt for a share or asset purchase. There can be some confusion between the two and, dependent on the business, there could be certain liabilities or benefits which make one better suited to your purchase or sale than the other.

At Gill Akaster we deal with both types regularly and thought it may be helpful to explain some of the main differences between them and the reasons for it. The accountancy and tax positions often vary hugely depending on which model is used but there are also significant legal differences that need to be considered.

Asset Purchase

Here, the buyer 'cherry picks' the items or assets of the business they wish to purchase. It is important to identify exactly what is being selected; such as machinery, stock, work in progress, premises, contracts, goodwill, etc. It is equally as important to identify which items are not going to be purchased such as existing creditors and debtors.

The main document will be an Asset Purchase Agreement and this will normally deal with some if not all of the following matters: -

• Premises - Freehold or leasehold property to be included and any possession or personal guarantee issues that need to be dealt with.

• Goodwill - The likelihood of repeat custom due to the goodwill the business has built up over time. This is often one of the most important assets purchased. Restrictive covenants are likely to be included so the seller cannot compete with the business for a set time frame in a given geographical area.

- Contracts - It's important to identify all contracts being purchased and to review their terms carefully. Any potential liabilities under the contracts will need to be checked and provisions included in the agreement to deal with these.

- Stock and Work in Progress - This must be identified early on and an agreed schedule drawn up at completion. Often this will be estimated given the constant fluctuation of these items within a business.

- Plant and Machinery - It is normal to have a detailed schedule setting out all physical pieces of plant and machinery to be purchased, with outlines of their current condition and any relevant lease or hire purchase agreements.

- Employees - When purchasing a business through an Asset Purchase, 'TUPE' legislation protects employees' rights on the transfer of the assets of the business. It is extremely important to identify which employees are to be automatically transferred to the buyer under TUPE regulations as there can be a high cost associated with them.

- Creditors and Debtors - These often remain with the seller so the buyer has a clean start.

- Intellectual Property - These assets have become more and more important over time and include trademarks, patents, registered designs, etc. It is important to identify these early on, as well as who owns them and to ensure there are formal assignments/transfers put in place so these go across to the buyer.

- VAT - If the business is purchased as a going concern then VAT will not be applicable as long as both parties are VAT registered.

- Warranties (Less extensive than in a share purchase, but there will still be warranties (statements) made by the seller in relation to the assets being sold. If any prove untrue then the buyer will have a potential warranty claim for any losses suffered)

Share Purchase

If the shares in the company who run the business are being acquired, then normally it will be the buyer's solicitors who prepare the initial documentation. This is because there will be extensive warranties and indemnities in the documentation to protect the buyer which makes it sensible for their solicitor to prepare them.

With a share purchase the buyer purchases the shares in a company from the shareholders and once these have been transferred, ownership of that company will pass to the buyer and will include any assets or liabilities. As the buyer is not 'cherry picking' assets then the potential for the buyer taking on liabilities is much greater.

The main document in a share purchase is a Share Purchase Agreement that, as well as dealing with the transfer of the ownership of the shares in the company, will deal with the following matters: -

- Completion Accounts - These are prepared immediately after completion and ensure both parties are aware of the company's financial position. Often the purchase price will be adjusted if the completion accounts are not exactly as anticipated.

- Restrictive Covenants - As with a share purchase the buyer will want to ensure the seller does not compete with them for a limited period of time in a certain geographical area. The period and area will depend on the size of the business and the area in which it operates. Careful consideration needs to be given to the drafting of these clauses – if drafted too wide then the court will class them as void and unenforceable.

- Indemnities - During the process of due diligence, if any significant issues are highlighted a specific indemnity against any related issues may be required to be given by the seller. This is more powerful than a warranty as the enforcement options for the buyer are much more extensive. Tax issues are often dealt with this way and, in larger transactions; there can be a separate detailed tax indemnity document. If any indemnities are broken, then the seller is under a duty to compensate the buyer accordingly.

- Schedules - Often attached to the Share Purchase Agreement will be several schedules, which will go into more detail in particular areas, such as any adjustments post-completion to the price or any future payments that are to be made that are conditional upon future performance of the company.

- Warranties - A large part of the Share Purchase Agreement will deal with warranties. These are statements made by the seller in relation to the company and are based on information gathered during the due diligence exercise. The purpose of a warranty is for the buyer to flush out any information that should be known before entering into a legally binding contract. This could include any litigation, hidden issues with the company or lower profitability than originally appeared.

There is much negotiation to the exact wording of the warranties given and the scope of them. The buyer will want wide and detailed warranties so they have a potential claim against the seller; the seller will not want to give any general warranties for fear of a future claim.

However, there are two means of protecting the seller. Firstly, there is the disclosure letter. This is a letter with supporting documents which is sent by the seller to the buyer and details the exceptions or qualifications to the warranties contained in the sale agreement. Secondly, there will often be a clause or schedule setting out limits on the potential liability of the seller in terms of value and time for any potential claims to be brought against them.

Although, in theory, if a warranty is found to be untrue, the buyer has a claim for damages against the seller, these are often very difficult and time consuming to prove. Therefore, it is always much better to make sure that the buyer carries out full and detailed due diligence of the target company, rather than rely on any potential breach of warranty claim)

The above outlines just some of the key legal differences between a Share Purchase and an Asset Purchase. There are of course many other areas that may be included depending on the complexity or the particular circumstances of the deal. Due to this complexity, guidance from a professional and experienced solicitor is essential to ensure you remain protected.

James Peterson
Gill Akaster LLP
www.gillakaster.com

Getting your house in order before a sale

Often shareholders wishing to sell give little priority to getting their "house in order" ahead of a sale and concentrate on the operational side of the business, and on growing sales and profits. But this should not be at the expense of corporate and legal housekeeping; overlooking this can lead to unwelcome price reductions once the buyer starts its due diligence and, in the worst case, the buyer walking away from the deal.

It is important to get advisers on board who have specialist experience in selling businesses. These will include business sales advisers, accountants, corporate lawyers and tax advisers, all of whom will be able to guide a seller in preparing for a sale, and then assist the seller on the transaction itself.

Although this may entail some time and cost, it is worthwhile starting to think about this well in advance of any sale process as a buyer is much more likely to be impressed, and prepared to pay a fuller price, if the Company is well organised, is on top of its internal administration, and has anticipated in advance any areas which may give a buyer cause for concern.

Once the sale process starts potential buyers and their advisers will want information from you quickly, but if this information is wrong or incomplete, this will undermine the buyer's confidence in you and the process generally.

Further down the line, a well advised buyer will require the seller to give warranties in respect of the business, and it is essential that the information provided is, so far as possible, accurate and not intentionally misleading, and when disclosing against the warranties, a seller should give as full and accurate disclosures as possible. Good preparation should enable a seller to do this.

So what sort of things, from a legal perspective, need to be looked at?

Statutory Books

It is surprising how many companies fail to maintain their statutory books, as required by the Companies Act, and some are not even aware of what or where they are! Although there is no legal definition of "statutory books", there is a definition of "company records" (which include the legally required register of members, register of directors and board minutes). A register of members is prima facie evidence of who the members of the Company are, and what shares they hold.

All companies must keep minutes of directors' meetings for ten years from the date of the meeting and copies of members' resolutions passed otherwise than at general meetings (which would include all written resolutions) and minutes of general meetings for ten years from the date of the resolution, decision or meeting. Likewise, all limited and unlimited companies, whether or not they are trading, must keep adequate accounting records.

A buyer will ask to see these as part of any due diligence exercise, so they should be complete and up to date, and reflect the current shareholdings and directorships. If these cannot be located or are incomplete this can lead to delays or a buyer refusing to complete until the position is rectified.

Seller's Due Diligence

Prior to any sale the buyer's solicitors will carry out a legal due diligence exercise (often alongside a financial review carried out by the Accountants). In advance of the sale process commencing it would be particularly advantageous therefore, from both a timesaving and housekeeping point of view, for a seller to gather together the relevant information and to ensure that all material matters are properly documented (and filed at Companies House, where appropriate) and are signed and dated. You should also talk to your tax advisers to make sure any potential sale will be structured in the most tax efficient way.

Typically this would cover areas such as the basic corporate history and current corporate information on the Company; the existing authorised and issued share capital and existing shareholders and details of any existing shareholders agreements; principal customers of and suppliers (including software and hardware) to the Company together with copy contracts (so that a review of such contracts can take place); details of the ownership of the Company's assets and identification of any liabilities; service contracts between the Company or any subsidiary company and the directors and employment details for all employees; material contracts of the business entered into by the Company or any group company, and where these are subject to change of control clauses; any governmental, legal or arbitration proceedings being threatened or brought by or against the Company or any subsidiary; and any arrangements which are not on an arm's length basis.

Key Contractual Documentation

A seller needs to clearly identify where the real value in the business lies, and how it is contractually protected. Often a Company will have entered into, or continued with, contractual commitments with third parties without written contracts having been put in place and/or without legal advice having been taken. Also it may be that the Company wants to reduce dependence on a particular customer or supplier, or that it is coming to the end of a lease on its property and it would be sensible for the Company to get any new arrangements agreed well in advance.

Ideally all critical contracts should be reduced to writing well in advance of any sale, so that a third party cannot take advantage of its position to unreasonably improve the terms, which might be the case if it is aware that the contract is crucial to a sale. For example, if a Company has important IP, checks should be made to ensure that the Company has full rights to use and exploit this.

Any change of control/early termination clause in any of these contractual arrangements needs to be carefully reviewed, to make sure these do not become a problem if the business is sold.

Don't forget key employees. The Company will need to have in place service agreements, particularly with the executive directors. Consideration should also be given to sensible incentive schemes to encourage key employees to stay with the business.

Lance Feaver
Keystone Law LLP
www.keystonelaw.co.uk

Warranty Woes

Having experienced the rollercoaster of emotions that can be involved in successfully selling a company or a business, a seller may be forgiven for taking some time out after completion to relax and enjoy the fruits of his labour. This sense of relief can quickly disappear however, if a seller is faced with a potential warranty or indemnity claim after completion.

During the course of a sale, whether of shares in a company or of assets, a seller would usually be expected to give certain warranties to the buyer. These are contractual statements about the business or company being sold. For example, a warranty might state that the company has not sold any defective products or that no employee has given notice to terminate his employment. Other common areas of warranty protection include tax affairs, commercial contracts, environment and intellectual property.

Whilst a buyer would be expected to conduct due diligence on the target company or business, this would be primarily aimed at ascertaining whether the target company or business is worth what he is paying for it. Warranties are intended to give the buyer some additional comfort regarding certain areas of the business and also give the buyer a remedy against the seller if any warranty given by the seller proves to be untrue.

A breach of warranty would generally give the buyer the right to sue the seller for breach of contract although the buyer would also usually be under a duty to mitigate his loss and more importantly, would need to show that the effect of the breach of warranty is to reduce the value of the acquired company or business.

This may be difficult to prove, particularly if the loss is solely down to management time (by tidying up a company's statutory books for example), which may not actually reduce the value of the company or business.

An indemnity on the other hand, is a promise by the buyer to compensate the seller for a particular, identifiable liability. For example, there will usually be a tax indemnity given by the seller for any tax liabilities of the target company which were not disclosed to the buyer in the accounts of the target company. A buyer may also require an indemnity in relation to certain environmental liabilities or any litigation that the company is involved in. Given the extent of the warranties in the acquisition agreement, a seller will usually seek to limit his liability in a number of different ways.

A seller will review the warranties in the acquisition agreement and make a list of any matters that conflict with any warranty in a disclosure letter. For example, if a warranty states that no employee has given notice to terminate his employment but two employees had given such notice, the seller would disclose this fact in the disclosure letter.

Generally, a buyer will not be able to claim against a seller for a breach of a warranty if the disclosure letter contains details of the particular fact or matter which conflict with that warranty.

Other ways for a seller to limit his liability under the warranties include:

• making the warranties subject to his awareness;

• putting time limits on warranty claims. This is usually anywhere between 18 and 36 months for non-tax warranties and 6 or 7 years for tax warranties since HM Revenue & Customs can reopen the tax affairs of companies up to six years after the end of the accounting period in which the tax event occurs; and

• putting financial limits on warranty claims, which would include the seller limiting his total liability under the warranties to the consideration he has received.

- Finally, it may even be possible to obtain warranty and indemnity insurance to cover any warranty claims. The premiums will usually depend on a number of factors including the value of the transaction, how complex it is and the nature of the warranties and indemnities. The insurers and their professional advisers will want to review the transaction documentation so it is important that sellers make contact with an insurance broker early enough so that all formalities can be dealt with.

If a potential claim comes to light, it is important for the parties and their professional to review the acquisition agreement and disclosure letter carefully to see whether any disclosures have been made by the seller against the warranty concerned and whether the seller's liability is limited in any way.

Following this, if the buyer still wishes to proceed with a claim, often full and frank communication with the seller and his professional advisers can result in any claim being settled out of court, saving both parties considerable costs.

Maung Aye
Mackrell Turner Garrett LLP
www.mackrell.com

They think it's all over – it's not yet!

After weeks or months of preparation and negotiation, you have finally done it. You have sold your business. You walk out of your solicitor's office with a smile on your face, a cheque in your pocket and a minor case of repetitive strain injury from signing 300 documents. You are ready for that well-earned rest.

But wait. There are a few things to think about first. If you have an earn out arrangement as part of the consideration, you will need to be sure that you know exactly what is required of you and that you keep on top of that. Know the key dates and the triggers for further payments becoming due, so that you don't let things slip.

If you have a consultancy agreement to provide ongoing services to the business you have sold, ensure you are clear on what you have to do and when. If you are staying on as a consultant or an employee in the business, you will also have a big mental task of adjusting to a new position – you will no longer be the boss and that is not always easy to accept. If you are staying, there may also be consequences if you leave in certain circumstances – being a 'Bad Leaver' could impact on your entitlement to consideration.

You will probably have signed restrictive covenants to prevent you competing with the business. Be very clear about what you are not allowed to do, and if in any doubt take advice again before you do anything which might conflict, otherwise you could find yourself in expensive litigation.

Most importantly, bear in mind that you will almost certainly have given warranties as part of the sale agreement. If any of those warranties are found to be untrue, a claim against you could follow. Even if you have put funds in escrow, or there has been a retention, against the possibility of claims, remember that if those funds are not enough to cover the claim, then you most likely remain liable for the rest. The warranties may last for two or three years (or seven for tax issues) and so it makes sense to know how long you have to wait before you are 'in the clear'. It is probably wise not to spend all the sale proceeds on a yacht the day after completion, just in case.

You will, hopefully, have been advised about all of these things as the sale has progressed, but it is easy to forget the detail in the euphoria (or relief) of completing the deal. Refresh your memory every so often by having a look through all those documents you signed, or get your lawyer to send you a checklist of the things, and dates, you need to be aware of.

Derek Rogers
Gardner Leader LLP
www.gardner-leader.co.uk

M&A Pricing Mechanisms

The Choices

The pricing mechanism used to determine the value of a target business will clearly have a significant effect on the actual price paid. Completion accounts have traditionally been used primarily as a way for a buyer to protect its investment. There has however, in recent years, been a move towards the use of a locked box structure.

Using a completion accounts mechanism, the buyer will pay a price based on an estimated value of assets and liabilities with that price being adjusted post completion once a full set of completion accounts have been prepared. Depending on the accuracy of the initial estimated value, the agreed payment terms and the complexity of the target business, there is therefore potential for the final price to be materially different to the expectation of the parties and also not known for some considerable time after completion.

Using a locked box structure generally means that the price payable is based on a recent historical balance sheet of the target and will not be adjusted save in respect of any agreed items of "leakage".

A summary of the main pros and cons of each mechanism is set out at the end of the article.

Choosing the Right Mechanism

The choice between the two mechanisms will depend on many factors such as market and sector conditions, financial stability of the target and the relative bargaining strength of the buyer and seller.

It is not quite as simple as saying that the completion accounts mechanism is always buyer friendly and locked box seller friendly. Both mechanisms have pros and cons for each party.

Timing is a key issue when considering the choice. Essentially, if using completion accounts, economic risk and benefit in the target pass to the buyer at completion, whereas with a locked box, economic risk passes at the agreed effective date before signing.

From a buyer's perspective, this means a lack of certainty as to achieving total value for the price it is paying. Therefore, the level of due diligence carried out by the buyer and its advisors will need to be sufficiently detailed to give it the comfort that the historic accounts upon which the price has been based were accurate and that the projected financial performance is realistically strong. Indeed, it is not uncommon for the buyer to request the seller to provide a financial due diligence report as a precursor to the price being fixed.

A level of certainty in respect of the final price to be paid is obviously paramount for both buyer and seller. From a seller's perspective, one of the key concerns about completion accounts is usually that a buyer will use the completion accounts process to "chip" away at the price post-completion. This is why the use of a locked box mechanism is attractive for sellers as there will be no pot completion adjustment to the price save for pre agreed "leakage".

Leakage

The parties will need to agree what constitutes "leakage" and "permitted leakage" in respect of the value of the business between the locked box accounts date and completion. Anything going beyond that will be dealt with by way of an indemnity from the seller to the buyer.

"Leakage" essentially means the transfer out of any value from the target business to the seller or its connected parties in the period between the locked box date and completion. The most obvious example is probably dividends but even the more indirect leakages are relatively easy to identify and agree (large salary increases for shareholder directors and intra-group

108

payments for example). Some payments, such as payment of staff wages and professional fees incurred in preparation for a business sale, may fall into a relatively grey area but it is usually possible to agree sensible "permitted leakages" which take into account the underlying reason for any payment.

Conclusions

Commercial considerations will often be paramount when making the decision on which mechanism to choose. The likely number of potential buyers interested in a transaction may affect the volume and quality of the information the seller is inclined to generate and release. Any risks or uncertainties about price or value accrued may be overtaken by the extent to which the buyer or seller values certainty at completion.

Buyers and sellers will want to minimise (i) the amount of management time spent on completion accounts; (ii) post transaction settling up negotiations; (iii) protracted negotiations as a result of complex sale and purchase agreements which may lead to the deal collapsing; and (iv) the risk of nasty surprises after completion.

More buyers and sellers can benefit from using a locked box, or from at least exploring what it might add to their transaction. With M&A market conditions modestly improving a locked box mechanism is one way to reduce some of the risks associated with a transaction and increase the likelihood that it will deliver the anticipated value.

Pros and Cons of Completion Accounts

Pros: Seller
Speed of execution as buyer may need less comfort of balance sheet before completion.

Seller will receive value for running the business right up until completion.

Pros: Buyer
Only pays for what it gets: price will be adjusted if business has deteriorated before completion

Ability to check completion accounts when in full control of business

Cons: Seller
Potential for dispute

Delay in ascertaining final price

Costs of preparation/review and any potential dispute

Cons: Buyer
Potential for dispute

Delay in ascertaining final price

Costs of preparation/review and any potential dispute

Pros and Cons of Locked Box

Pros: Seller
Certainty of price

Cost. No completion accounts mechanism results in cost savings

Pros: Buyer
Certainty of price

Cost. No post-completion adjustment results in cost savings

Cons: Seller
Will not get full benefit from continued operation of business in the interim period

Cons: Buyer
Increased reliance on warranties and comfort on balance sheet; enhanced due diligence often necessary

Risk of business deteriorating between locked box date and completion

Jonathan Williamson
(Formerly OCS Solicitors LLP)
Now Blandy & Blandy LLP
www.blandy.co.uk

Management reporting – it's not all about the financial

Managing a business involves a range of disciplines and not all of those involved in decision making will have financial expertise. Financial accounts comprising numbers squeezed on to an illegible single page or as part of a complex 8-page pack is unlikely to be read or helpful.

Whilst the finance department is likely to have responsibility for producing management information it cannot be done in isolation if it is to be meaningful and, rather than just providing numbers, guide the user through them.

Management Reporting that properly explains past performance and informs decision making will consider:

- capturing, processing and analysing data (financial and nonfinancial) in a way that is appropriate to the business.
- comparing results to plan/forecast with appropriate management discussion to confirm validity. Variances will also help to update future forecasts when appropriate.
- identifying KEY numerical information clearly from within the overall information presented.
- including key data that explains/drives the financial performance. This may be financial ratios, staff related, productivity information or whatever is relevant to an individual business.
- WORDS. All management reporting should include words, based on the evidence, which can be understood by all those involved in decision making.

Caroline Billington
A-count-a-bility Ltd
www.a-count-a-bility.co.uk

Does Your Business Have Valuable IPR and Are You Maintaining It?

IPR can take various forms in any business and proper protection can substantially increase the value of your business. You should regularly consider and manage your IPR portfolio, including:

Patent: registered right usually for 20 years for novel non-obvious inventions capable of industrial application. Registration is territorial and grants monopoly rights in respect of that invention. These have been worth (and infringement has cost) £millions to mobile phone companies recently.

Trade mark: a logo or other sign or gesture that is distinctive and non-descriptive and not identical to or confusingly similar with another's mark. They should be registered to provide monopoly rights in the relevant sector and again are territory specific. They can be renewed indefinitely and a properly protected brand can add significant value to a business.

Copyright: unregistered right that arises automatically. It is not a monopoly right as it only protects against copying, not independent similar creation, but can last up to 70 years from year of death of the creator (depending on the type of copyright). This can be very relevant to software, artwork, proofs and databases.

Design right: registered and unregistered rights to protect the appearance of a novel distinctive 3D object. Can last up to 25 years in the UK and is important to things such as designer furniture equipment and ornaments (but not spare parts).

Confidential information: unregistered right in information that is of a confidential nature. This can cover a lot of sensitive business information, such as finance models and customer lists, of fundamental value to a business.

The cost of protecting your IPR is more than out-weighed by the value associated with this intangible business asset.

Austin Blackburn
Nash & Co. Solicitors
www.nash.co.uk

VIMBOs explained

Owner managers with successful businesses approaching retirement are faced with a number of options. One is to sell the business to a third party buyer, in which case they would need the guidance of a firm like Evolution CBS to source the buyers.

However, in some situations, the owner may prefer to give the management team the chance to acquire the business. This may be the case where a number of the following factors apply:

1. the owner wants to retain an interest;

2. management have helped grow the business and are at a stage where they are ready to take the helm;

3. the owner does not want to conduct a sales process and alert customers and competitors to the fact that the business is on the market;

4. it is not a business where there are natural third party buyers;

5. the owner is prepared to take his consideration over a number of years.

Where these factors do apply, there is a process with the strange acronym of a VIMBO, which stands for a Vendor Initiated Management Buy Out, which can meet the goals of the owner and manager.

In a VIMBO, the management team set up a new company which buys the existing company. The owner is effectively paid out of retained cash in the business and from the profits of the company over the next few years. However, as the money is being paid for the sale of the shares rather than being paid as a dividend, the owner may be able to benefit from Entrepreneurs Relief and pay only 10% tax.

The reasons for using this route are:

1. the owner can realise the value of his business;

2. there is no need to find a third party purchaser;

3. it is tax efficient for the owner and company;

4. it incentivises managers;

5. it allows the owner to retain an interest and control;

6. it devolves ownership to managers.

Ian Brent
Fladgate LLP
www.fladgate.com

Due diligence issues on selling a business with an IP asset base

Anyone acquiring or investing in a business will want to know what intellectual property (IP) is included in the target's assets and to what extent this is the engine for generating revenue. A business which is being prepared for sale should make sure that it will have ready answers to the enquiries which the purchaser's lawyer will make.

The first step is to identify the IP rights which exist. These could include registered and/or unregistered rights. Patents are registered rights. Certain rights, such as copyright, are not capable of registration in the UK. Other rights such as trademarks and design rights can exist in both registered and unregistered form.

Searching and verifying ownership of registered rights

To develop an effective IP due diligence strategy, it is important to first understand what IP assets are most significant to the business and any future deal, any key markets and what products (if any) are in the pipeline.

It is important to ensure proper chain of title for each right and whether there are any joint ownership issues which could complicate post-completion matters. Does any other party have a right to the IP or are any rights subject to a commercial co-existence agreement?

It is very common for a business to use third party sub-contractors or freelancers to create software or artwork. It is essential that the contractual chain can be established so that appropriate warranties can be given that the business is the owner when the time comes.

These are some of the things a business can do to prepare:

- Obtain and review copies of all agreements related to IP and technology to check the terms thoroughly and in particular, if any third party to IP is integral to the business consider if any agreements contain restrictive assignment terms or 'change of control' provisions.

- Consider writing an intellectual property policy to set out guidelines which address:

- New work, inventions and other developments which should be routinely assessed at predetermined milestones.

- When to include lawyers and patent attorneys to register rights.

- The approach to third party infringements or potential threats to IP.

If a business takes these steps at a time before it is under intense pressure in relation to achieving a sale or investment, it can maximise the value of IP and have an impact on the price which can be achieved.

Kim Walker
Thomas Eggar
www.thomaseggar.com

Exit strategies don't have to be complicated

With the economy picking up from the global downturn, business owners who have weathered the financial storm have come out on the other side with businesses which are much more robust, and are now in a position to achieve successful exits from their businesses. Having a clear exit strategy doesn't have to be complicated and it will define the key stages of the sale process.

Share or asset sale?

The first distinction to make is whether the shares in the company are to be sold or simply certain assets.

With a company limited by shares, the individual shareholders of the company can choose to sell their shareholdings or the company itself may simply choose to sell some or all of its assets.

When purchasing the assets of a company, you can pick and choose which assets to buy, specifically excluding any liabilities. Conversely, buying all the shares in a company will result in any liabilities and obligations remaining with the company, whether you know about them or not. You may however, be able to negotiate the exclusion of certain company liabilities in the share purchase agreement.

Due Diligence

As a buyer, it is important, whether on a share or an asset sale, to know as much as possible about the business you are purchasing. This means instructing lawyers, accountants and any other relevant experts to review any documentation relating to the target business or company.

The due diligence review is usually instigated by the prospective buyer sending a due diligence questionnaire to the seller or his lawyers with numerous questions around the business' performance, its contracts, its relationship with its employees, its intellectual property and any litigation it is involved in. The seller will provide replies and documentation to the buyer and his team who will then look through and review each document in turn, looking out for any points of concern.

In certain circumstances it may be appropriate to request an indemnity to cover a specific liability uncovered during the due diligence process.

Negotiations and process

Negotiations often start with the buyer and seller entering into "Heads of Terms". These are important as they outline the agreed terms between the parties which will then be transposed into a formal agreement for the purchase of the business or company. They are usually non-binding, save for certain exceptions and often include "lock-out" provisions which prevent a party from negotiating a better deal with a third party for a certain period, and restrictive covenants to ensure that if the deal does not proceed, each party cannot poach any of the other party's employees.

The next stage is for the lawyers to draft an agreement incorporating the terms which the parties have agreed, including how the purchase price is to be paid (whether all up front or deferred for example).

This agreement will be legally binding and will usually include certain warranties and indemnities which the seller will give the buyer about the business. The warranties are essentially statements which will give the buyer a right to sue the seller for breach of contract if they prove to be untrue. For example, the seller may warrant that there is no litigation affecting any intellectual property is owned by the company.

118

The agreement will also include certain limits on the seller's liability so that the seller can be certain of his maximum exposure for a successful claim against him by the buyer under the agreement. The seller will also have a chance to inform the buyer of any matter which may conflict with or contradict any of the warranties in a disclosure letter. Generally, a buyer will not be able to claim against the seller for a breach of a warranty if the matter giving rise to the breach has been fairly disclosed in the disclosure letter.

Other strategies

Selling your company or business is just one way of achieving an exit but this may not be the right decision for you. If your business is not achieving the growth you would want, you may wish to consider entering into a joint venture or collaboration with like-minded businesses with expertise in different but complementary areas.

This could provide you with access to an entirely new client base in order to expand and grow your business. It may also be a good idea to think about whether any existing shareholders' agreement has adequate protections for the shareholders on exit. Many companies will draft these early on and they may no longer be appropriate for your business today.

Maung Aye
Mackrell Turner Garrett LLP
www.mackrell.com

The Value of Knowing Your Numbers

The following article is a basic insight into why knowing your numbers is important and what numbers are the most useful to start with – it is by no means a definitive list, more a practical and pragmatic view of what you need in place to run your company effectively.

What is the first thing that comes to mind when you think of when you look at your company's financials? Apart from the number at the bottom line!

You need to know how your accounts are made up. You need to be instructing your accountant to build you accounts how you want them presented.

Some business owners I've met don't understand their numbers – this leads to all sorts of problems. Typically, the financial bod ends up running the company.

There are some people who truly have a fear of money, as some do of spiders.   The fear of money is termed Chrometophobia.

Assuming that you are not in that category, I often hear that numbers cause you concern. The good news is that it is probably more simple than you think – It's about recording and understanding what it all means.

Maybe it is obvious; the best business model is to have an income greater than the outgoings.

As Charles Dickens wrote:

"Annual income twenty pounds, annual expenditure nineteen [pounds] nineteen [shillings] ad six [pence], result happiness. Annual income twenty pounds, annual expenditure twenty pounds ought [zero shillings] and six [pence], result misery."
Mr Micawber from David Copperfield.

If you don't know the financial numbers of your business, how would you know you are making any money, or more worryingly, running out of cash.

I've heard various reasons why business owners don't know their numbers... 'I can't understand the terminology'/ 'it's boring; I leave it to my accountant' / 'it's too complicated'.

One of the best one's I've heard is...
'My accountant tells me how we're doing at the end of the financial year!'

Your accountant doesn't know how well you're doing. They can tell what you've done in the past – Statutory accounts are history, the P&L (Profit and Loss) is theory anyway. The P&L is just a snapshot in time.

Warren Buffet, known as 'the Sage of Omaha' one of the world's most successful businessmen said *"if you don't know the score, you can't tell the winners from the losers."*

So let's look at why numbers are important.

Think of a game of Golf, or Football; or any game that scores points. You know you are winning when you have more points than your opponents. It's the same in business. You need to be scoring more money in than the business is paying out. It's just that the income and outgoings have more places to come from and go to. A place for everything and everything in its place.

To see if you are keeping on track, monitor the rate of income versus costs. As a barometer shows you whether the weather has changed and what is happening; checking spend versus income, gives an indication of the health of your business.

Some big retailers monitor this on an hourly basis, whereas many SMEs would find weekly/monthly figures more useful.

I know one business where the owner has a dial on their PC screen. It simply shows if they are in the red or black on a real-time basis.

Knowing your numbers is also a good motivator. Both good and bad results will motivate. Think how it would be for you to be able to share with your team that the business did well this week/month/year. Or, conversely, think of a sales team that need to hit a target next week and they are behind. I bet a lot of work would go on to land those deals.

Numbers are universally understood across the business world. When you understand numbers, you can assess how well a company in China is performing against a company in the UK, or anywhere in the world.

The success of a small business can be compared with that of a larger business. It about the percentages. For example, it may be that a large corporate is making massive profits in real-terms, but a small percentage profit against the investment. A small business may actually be making a better return; for every pound in, a great rate of return. So, you can see that you need to know your numbers to determine which company is doing best.

A forward looking budget helps a business assess how well it could do. To get a realistic view of the potential rate of growth, a company needs to know the numbers from previous years. Many investors will want the management accounts from the last 3 years, as a minimum, to see how the company has done so far. Previous successes are a reflection on past decisions.

When making business decisions, it is more than helpful to know the numbers. Apart from the history of progress, you need to know whether there are going to be enough funds to support growth and investment; at least to pay the wages for 'x' months. If a business is struggling, it is imperative that the decision maker knows what the numbers are to make sure the business does not go over it's available credit. It is more usual for a company to go broke whist in profit.

As I've heard Rob Goddard say, many times, *"You can make a loss many times. You can only run out of money once!"*

I hope you would agree that, as a business owner, you should know what your business is about and what's going on in it. After all, you wouldn't want to fly with an airline whose captain, on welcoming you to the plane, noticed the cockpit and exclaimed, 'oh my god, what a lot of dials and controls. That's scary!' or, if you heard your doctor say that your blood pressure was 5000 over 4 (120 over 80 is considered about right). I think I would want a proper doctor who knew the numbers.

One thing that often confuses is the language used by accountants and financial people. When you learn the buzz-words it becomes so much easier. They are not complicated, just different and need translating.

Let's focus on the basics: The Balance Sheet, Profit and Loss, Cashflow Forecast and Managements Accounts.

The Balance Sheet:

The balance sheet is really just a view of...

- Things and Stuff – e.g. cash, stock, money owed by customer, business premises, intellectual property and goodwill.

This needs to equal what the business...

- Owes – e.g. bank loan, money owed to suppliers and tax due.
  and
- Owns – e.g. the money you put in and the profit kept in the company's bank account.

Profit and Loss:

This shows how much money the company made (or lost) for a given year. It is only theory as it's a snapshot in time. It doesn't take into account the fact that you just made a great sale – if it is outside the date range... or that you're just about to pay a massive bill. It also doesn't take into account the Tax bill or VAT.

Some business owners forget to hold enough cash in a reserve account to pay the Taxes. This puts a huge strain on the business cash flow. That's another reason to know your numbers.

Cashflow Forecast:

Cash flow is the movement of money in and out of your business. A positive trend (increasing bank balance) shows you are bringing in more than you are spending. A declining trend indicates you may be running out of money.

To create a forecast, you need to know the actual costs anticipated for the month/year going forward and input the known incomes along with the target sales forecasts.

This will give an overview forecast to show you,

1. when the actual cash will run out (reality), and

2. how the numbers will look, when the forecasted income is received.

A key number is the bottom credit line. What is the maximum credit available, how far are you from it at any time and are you heading towards or away from it?

Management Accounts:

Management accounts are used to plan and control a business. They are also used to help make the decisions on how the business will be run.

They can cover any period e.g. retailers often have daily management information on sales, margins and stock levels.

The more accurate and current the numbers you have for your business, impacts on the usefulness of the management accounts.

124

For example, a couple of key numbers are:

Profit Margin - how much money was made for the sale after taking away costs; usually tracked as a percentage for comparison.

Total income for the day/week/month verses the total costs – Did you make more money for the day than it cost to run the business? This is often expressed as an actual figure supported by a percentage.

These often form part of an overall KPI (Key Performance Indicators) program to monitor the progress of the company.

To know at when your business has moved into actual profit, you need to know the Break-Even point. This information is also used to monitor the size of the profit (or loss).

Another important number is to understand your Maximum Utilisation. It is easy to take on more business than your company can cope with, and not be able to keep up with the schedule for delivery. Be clear on how many hours your team are working, against how many you have available. If you have a shortfall, you can take on more work.

When it comes to cash in the business, there are three types: - Operating, Investing and Financing.

Operating Cash is the money you have retained in the business; that you can use to run the business and buy stock, for example. Useful numbers are, how much money do we need to keep going for another month/year and pay all the bills and salaries.

Investing Cash is used in the same way as Operating Cash, but it comes as an input form the business owner or an investor. This money needs to be paid back at some agreed point. If you use your savings, make sure you can earn more from your business than you would get from a building society.

Financing Cash is the most expensive, usually in the form of a loan from the bank. This money will require interest to be paid for too. Often there is also an 'administration' fee to pay. Make sure you know your numbers so you can see that the return will more than cover the loan. A loan that requires a monthly payment also affects cash flow. When things get tight, the banks tend not to wait too long before chasing for their money.

If you have a Cash Gap, understand how much it's costing you.

Some businesses add a percentage to their invoices to cover the effective loan to the customer for late payment.

Typically, the cash gap is the time from when you paid for stock to when you get paid for the products you made/supplied.

Apart from the agreed cash gap, poor payment is like poison to SMEs. This is the amount of days that your invoice is outstanding beyond the agreed payment date. This is how many extra days' credit you have allowed your customer; and unless you are a bank charging interest, it's your money. Collect it!

I've found that some business owners abdicate responsibility for their financials, then wonder why they are in trouble. Take ownership of the bookkeeping and delegate to a professional, when you can. Make sure you collect all the numbers you need to run your business effectively.

Typically, the owners of SMEs have never had training on financials, they started a business and got going. Often brilliant at the business itself, but lacking in experience and training on the boring bit.

Get your financials right, and running the business becomes so much more controlled.

Alex Petty
Alexpetty.biz
www.alexpetty.biz

WHAT IS EVOLUTION?

Business Sales Advisors

Selling your business is likely to be one of the most important decisions that you make in your life. Therefore choosing the right business sales broker and agent to represent you and work on your behalf is crucial.

Evolution's team of professional sales advisers have one aim; that you experience a smoothly run selling and transfer process, which culminates in you being sure that you sell your business for all it's worth.

At the heart of this is our proven five stage business sale methodology. Selling a business is a sales and marketing led process, not a financial one. It's about attracting strategic buyers and placing them in a competitive market, so that price and exit terms are enhanced for your advantage. There is no set valuation for a particular business. There are a multitude of factors that affect price – historic profit is only a small one!

It is also critical that the important areas of tax efficiency, protection of intellectual property, integration of systems & processes and wealth management are considered thoroughly too. Evolution will provide you with professionals in these fields so that you benefit from expert advice and guidance. Our goal is that you not only maximize the value of your business but that you maintain your wealth.

It has been calculated that in excess of 1,000 hours are spent during an average ten-month cycle to sell a business. Evolution, as an experienced business sales broker and agent, will take that burden from you so that you can continue to run your business in the safe knowledge that the sale is in the hands of experienced professionals.

Testimonials

Don't take our word for it.
Hear from people we have helped...

Greatly impressed by your breadth of knowledge
"I first saw Rob and his team 'in action' at one of their Masterclasses and was greatly impressed by their breadth of knowledge and down to earth attitude."

Phil Hayes, CEO, Management Futures

Rob knows his profession
"At our very first meeting with Rob, it came across that we were dealing with a person who knows his profession well, and explains it in a very informal and comfortable way."

Anthony Browne, Director, St John's Wood Interiors Ltd

We are very pleased
"We are very pleased with the service you provided and will keep you in mind should we ever need your services in the future."

Aneesa Verjee-Lorenz, MSc, PharmaQuest Ltd

Critical in terms of exit value
"Having Rob's team handle the marketing process has enabled me to continue running and growing the business over the past 10 months which has proven to be critical in terms of exit value."

David Gould, CEO, Canby Ltd

Great value for money
"You provide a great value for money 'hands-on' business service to Owner Managed Businesses and private clients looking to exit their businesses in what are difficult financial conditions."

Jim Blake, Accountant

Innovative thinking and great problem solving skills

"...an enviable breadth of commercial skills and experience and an often disarming approach to situations, making your company highly effective. This, coupled with innovative thinking and great problem solving skills, has made your business a 'must have' solution."

M Whittle, Commercial Director, DTP Group

Extremely professional and positive

"Fantastic service matched by expertise and integrity. Your company is extremely professional and positive, and has always found a way to help me through the process. I would recommend to others: their business guidance to clients looking to sell is invaluable."

A Petty, Managing Director, TGWC Ltd

No hesitation in recommending their services

"They understand the needs of their client, take time to consider various options and suggest a pragmatic way forward. I would have no hesitation in recommending their services."

R Giles, Director, RDP Associates Inc.

Very impressed with your advice and your service

"We were very impressed with your advice and your service and we will certainly recommend you to our contacts here that are looking for advice."

John and Jenny Perkins Provost of Masdar Institute and Marketing Manager of Emirates Advanced Investments

A comfort and a pleasure dealing with you

"...a great relief to both Heather and I. Thank you for selling the business for us and it has been a comfort and a pleasure dealing with you"

Anthony Record, CEO, Oswald Record Group

Stewart Alban 9Y1AZ.

P·41